CTRL ALT SURVIVE

The Secrets of My
Small Business Succcess

Nathan Phinney

FIRST EDITION, OCTOBER 2024

© 2024 Nathan Phinney

All Rights Reserved.

Published in the United States by Convilo, LLC

ISBN: 9798339896753

www.ctrlaltsurvive.com

Printed in the United States of America

10 9 8 7 6 5 4 3 2 1

For Doug, who fostered my interest in audio production and ham radio, and gave me the Canon XL-1 video camera that I carried around the world in several adventures that are detailed in these pages. That camera helped me support my nascent family while I gradually figured out how to be a grownup. His profound generosity and love of neighbor inspired me to be generous to others and to look out for people who need help.

I think he would hate this attention, but might have loved this book.

CONTENTS

1. The Bear Who Wanted To Be A Bear.................1
2. Talking Cars and Helicopters 13
3. California...19
4. Dabbawalas..28
5. Riding The Jet Ski......................................43
6. The Price Is Right......................................53
7. Focus..64
8. The Sorcerer's Apprentice............................78
9. Failure Is Optional.....................................94
10. You Can Buy Customers 101
11. The Irish Goodbye....................................107
12. Walking Each Other Home.........................119
Acknowledgements.......................................128

Chapter 1

THE BEAR WHO WANTED TO BE A BEAR

"We are thieves, stealing glimpses of an American dream that we can never achieve. Welcome home. Swim into the ocean, drown in your devotion. We refuse to compromise. We had to get it right."
— *Hideous Supermodels*

My mother shopped at garage sales most weekends when I was a little boy. Often, she selected for me another child's discarded treasure, like some GoBots, which are unlicensed knockoffs of Hasbro's Transformers, re-imagined to be more compatible with poverty, or a plastic replica of Luke Skywalker's landspeeder with two out of three air-cooled thrust turbines still intact.

On another occasion, she brought home a book, *The Bear Who Wanted To Be A Bear* by Jörg Steiner, which was an odd sort of vaguely socialist parable about a bear who woke up from hibernation to the sounds of a factory being constructed above his den. The factory management is skeptical of the bear's claim of being a bear, and they insist that he must stop being a "lazybones" and must shave and punch a time clock and get to work in the factory. The illustrations are comically dystopian and more than a little bit Soviet, and I won't spoil the ending for you, but the bear finds himself wrestling with questions of identity, meaning, and purpose.

I lied to you. I'm totally going to spoil the ending. Eventually the bear gets laid off, and that ends up being a good thing, because he subsequently wanders in to a hotel, and the clerk at the front desk refuses to rent him a room because they don't allow bears, so he suddenly remembers that he is, in fact, a bear, and joyfully goes back to his den to sleep through the rest of the winter. It is an above average children's book.

I had the fortune of traveling to Gliwice, Poland once. My first job out of college was at a Fortune 500 engineering and construction company that was started by John "Si" Fluor in Santa Ana, California in 1912. I started in the marketing department, and one of my assignments was to make propaganda videos about how terrific global outsourcing was. I liked to travel, and I had a video camera, so they sent me to capture footage in glamorous oil and gas producing places like Oklahoma, Illinois, Louisiana, and Texas, but also to the Philippines, China, India, and Poland.

I prepared for my trip to Gliwice by learning 30 phrases in Polish that I thought might be important. Phrases like "Dziękuję" (Thank you) and "Dzień dobry" (Hello), but also some fun ones like "Czy mówisz po angielsku?" (Do you speak English?) and "Niestety, nie mówię po polsku," which I hope means "Regrettably, I do not speak Polish."

I got there a day early, and in contrast to much of Europe,

war-torn Gliwice is not a place where English is reliably understood by the populace, but I delighted in exploring the city, armed with my thirty poorly pronounced and mostly useless phrases. I ordered food by pointing at a menu item without knowing what it was, (delicious, but I still couldn't tell you) and I wandered the beautiful town square where I enjoyed some very good Tyskie and Zywiec beer.

When my hosts eventually arrived, one of whom turned out to be Dutch, we went back to the town square and I discovered that they were all very curious about Americans. I remember we were drinking this sort of prune flavored liquor called Slivovitz (or Śliwowica in Polish) which might have been serviceable as a substitute for gasoline. They asked me what Americans considered to be strong liquor, and I lamely said something about Jägermeister, which I had never tried, but assumed to be strong based on contextual clues, and they laughed hysterically. One of them said that his grandma uses it as cough syrup.

Another one of them wanted to show me photos from her trip to America, which turned out to be mostly palm trees, people wearing U.S. flag themed apparel, and several rather ordinary looking pickup trucks with lift kits and large tires. It was fascinating to see America through her eyes, but something about these engineers struck me in the same way our questionable transportation choices apparently struck them. Every time I said "tell me about yourself" or "what do you do?" they never said one word about their careers.

Instead, they said things like "I'm a skier" or "I'm really just a family man" or "My obsession right now is backpacking." It made me begin to wonder why Americans universally describe their identity from a sense of vocation. Ask an American to tell you about himself, and he might say "I'm a dentist" or "I make terrible propaganda videos about global outsourcing."

I realized that I wanted to be like them, to have a sense of self that wasn't exclusively about how I paid my bills. Perhaps, like the bear in the hotel who wanted to be a bear, I was on to something. I wanted to find out who I was outside of work. I realized, in that town square in Poland, that to do that – to have a different outcome than everyone else, I was going to have to make some different choices than my peers and learn to embrace risk. That was the seed that grew into years of attempted entrepreneurship, and eventually a business. I didn't want a ceiling on how much money I was allowed to make, because I wanted to someday earn the right to *be* more than my *job*.

In the fall of 2009, I was having dinner in a Chinese buffet restaurant with two old friends. We agreed that IT services were ripe for disruption, and had a few half baked ideas that we imagined were disruptive. I remember saying, "What if we can do this for ten years and then sell it for a life changing amount of money?" We defined that as a number with at least two commas in it, and all decided it was a fantastic idea, so I quit my job in Las Vegas and moved back to Southern California on New Year's Day, 2010, with my wife Kelly and a three month old baby boy in tow.

We each deposited $800 into a Bank of America business checking account, and filed for incorporation in California with the help of our new accountant, Larry. We celebrated at a mediocre sushi restaurant and I nearly got into my first bar fight.

It was terrifying and exhilarating. I felt alive and anxious and determined. I will resist the urge to leave you in suspense. One of my co-founders left the company on good terms in 2016, and my remaining partner and I achieved the outcome we had dreamed about, ten years and seven months later, to the day. It was an incredible thing to be a part of.

Together, we worked to build a company that served customers around the nation, through fits and starts, scrap by scrap, until it earned recognition by both Ingram Micro and CRN, ranking it as one of the top 500 IT Managed Service Providers in North America.

We started with a vision that wasn't fully formed. A jumble of half-truths and even some wildly misguided beliefs that made our failure almost inevitable. But here's the thing—we were lucky, because some of our other ideas incrementally pushed us forward. Every chapter of this book dissects one of those ideas, those advantages we didn't know we had, which when stacked up, helped us arrive at an inflection point where someone was willing to send us an embarrassingly large wire transfer in exchange for what we had built.

I'm really not here to flex. The heroes of this story are our employees and our customers. They gave me reasons to want to be better at this and inspired me every day. This is also a story about some uncomfortable truths—what it really takes to build and run a company, and how we did it. I intend to spill some tea about the screw-ups, the sleepless nights, and the moments when self-doubt claws at your throat.

Being in charge, most of the time, feels less like steering a ship and more like duct-taping a leaky hull. Leadership is less about control and more about learning, over and over, that you really don't have much, and figuring out a way to move forward anyway.

This is also a story about letting go.

Not long after the IT business sold, I escaped to Nashville for a few days with my friend Carl. I brought my guitar because we were hoping to write a song. It wasn't the first time. Twenty years earlier, we had been paired up to write music together in a songwriting class at the Contemporary Music Center on Martha's Vineyard. Out of that forced collaboration came Salvadoreña—a melodramatic acoustic rock number that sounded a little like Dashboard Confessional crooning about a displaced janitor who had the misfortune of walking past us while we were looking for inspiration. We found out later she was really from Guatemala, but "Guatemalteca" didn't roll off the tongue the same way, so we took some artistic license.

We spent several days in Nashville writing the song that became Devotion. Serendipitously, our old drummer Paul happened to be in town, so we brought him along too. I take strange pleasure in naming things. We named our band Hideous Supermodels, a name I chose in homage to a C.S. Lewis novel, *That Hideous Strength*, and because it strikes a delicious balance between being pretentious, meaningless, and yet unmistakably memorable. A hideous supermodel, I opined, is a person of average beauty, just like a tiny giant is a person of average size. The words neutralize one another. I like a name that doesn't apologize for existing. Admit it, you're curious what that music sounds like.

Carl was moderately successful in the music industry, and by moderately successful I mean he had written and recorded some songs that charted on college radio, and we all admired him because he received a record deal with "tour support" which essentially means his record label paid for a van so that he and his band could travel around the country to festivals during his twenties playing very loud music for the enjoyment of very sweaty teenagers, and then billed that cost against the profits from their subsequent album, committing him to a life of indentured servitude and gas station hot dogs. Incidentally, if you're ever considering signing a recording contract, you might want to ask an attorney to explain it to you first.

On that same trip, I also had a chance to meet T Bone Burnett, who produced two of my favorite albums of all time (*August and Everything After* by Counting Crows and *Bringing Down The Horse* by The Wallflowers) and spend some time with my friend Tom Willett, who founded the Contemporary Music Center, later served as President of Dark Horse Institute, and previously ran A&R for a division of Sony Music, where he worked with several artists I grew up listening to, including Phil Keaggy, Al Green, Wynton Marsalis, Sam Phillips, Tonio K, and Amy Grant. It was a great week that left me feeling inspired and refreshed.

Though I'd sold the business and was now settling into my new life as a platinum card carrying member of the American middle class, the weight of the struggle to get there lingered like a hangover. There was this tension, a feeling I couldn't quite shake, so I brought that to the song. For the vocals, I decided to use this quirky analog effect called the Vocoder. It showed up on the scene in the seventies but was popularized more recently by Daft Punk and Kanye West. The Vocoder does something fascinating—it takes whatever you sing and spits it back at you in a pitch-perfect, robotic tone. It's cold, it's mechanical, but also weirdly mesmerizing. The sound reminds me of what people in 1980 thought robots in the year 2000 would sound like.

It sneaks up on you, a whisper at first, barely there, until the robots aren't just in the background—they're harmonizing with us. By the end, they take over completely, snarling the last line of the song soullessly, polished to the point of sterility. As the vocoder replaced our singing, I found myself thinking about those imperfections—the cracks and pitch shifts that remind us we're listening to something human. There's a kind of beauty in that mess, and it's the first thing to disappear when we ask technology to "fix" what was never meant to be flawless.

Perfection seems like a good goal, but achieving it feels more like erosion, slowly devouring the coastline until there's nothing left but smooth, open water.

See, these are the kind of thoughts that accompany what they call "burnout." It creeps in when you've spent years on autopilot, stretched too thin, chasing too much. It's no mystery how I ended up here. In 2020, I was running an IT service provider, juggling SOC2 Type II reports with hundreds of documentation requests, trying to keep sales revenue on track while making sure we could meet payroll.

I was still doing some service calls, training a team that was exhausted and under-appreciated, applying for a PPP loan, calming panicked clients, wrestling with a relentless ticket queue, and in the middle of it all, trying to sell the business, with all of the diligence and documentation that entails. Then the pandemic hit full throttle. The schools shut down. And my wife, Kelly, lost her job when the family-owned boat manufacturer where she'd worked for years as a bookkeeper decided to close its doors for good.

I'm not sure if I needed a barista or a therapist. I picked "barista."

But before all of that could happen, the business needed a name. One of my deepest, darkest secrets is that I have never cared much about computers. I'm from the tail end of Gen X, the first generation that grew up with personal computers, and to me they always seemed omnipresent and underutilized. I like efficiency and opportunity. I also really like helping people, and the people around me always seemed to not understand computers very well. Over and over again, I found myself saying, "we could spend a lot more time at Del Taco if we design our high school yearbook with software instead of grease pencils" and "if we network these computers together, all the engineers could send jobs to the plotter at the same time, and we can play Warcraft 2 while we wait for everything to print." Later on I said, "if we just modify these registry keys, IBM Tivoli will tell our boss that we are at an acceptable level of productivity and utilization, so that we can leave early for happy hour."

I knew I was bright in some sense, but never by any meaningful metric a "genius" like those guys who fix computers at the mall, so I surrounded myself with two of the smartest and most trustworthy people I knew. I met Chad in middle school, and remembered that he had executed a few self-started business ideas and admired the way he ran operations and accounting for his family's landscaping business. He would run our back office, procurement, payroll, human resources, accounts payable and receivable. The other fellow, Chris, had already worked as an IT director for several years and has forgotten more about technology than I will ever know. I still count them both among the smartest and best people I've ever known.

A book about starting a business by Guy Kawasaki suggested there is value in names that leverage an alliteration, early in the alphabet, which made sense to me. Later at a charity auction, our company's logo appeared at the top of an alphabetized list of sponsors, way above U.S. Bank at the very bottom, and I knew that was good advice.

I also became aware of an A.C. Nielsen study of wine labels. It turns out that wine labels with an animal on them outsell wine labels with no animal on them by a ratio of something like three to one. In 2010, if you walked down the wine aisle in the supermarket, you'd see lots of frogs and goats and ducks and dogs, so I wanted an alliterative reference to an animal, early in the alphabet, that communicated the right things about us.

So, Bright Bear Technology Solutions was what we decided to call it. It ended up working out well, because everyone had their own idea about what the name meant.

People in Chicago thought it was great that we were named after the Chicago Bears. A real estate developer in Costa Mesa was certain that we were named for his Alma Mater, the Cal Bears of U.C. Berkeley, and a lot of people thought the bear in our logo looked a bit like the one on the California state flag. To some decision makers, the bear was cute. To others, it was strong. To others, they thought we might have been a paint company, but everyone seemed to be able to remember it. In a sea of companies that were named things like 'Initrode Xteklitron,' designed to demonstrate that the IT guys are smarter than you are, our name was easy to spell, and our branding and presentation was unintimidating. We realized later that this posture made our customers feel like *they* were the smart ones, for hiring us.

2

TALKING CARS AND HELICOPTERS

"Michael, I believe in good and evil, and I must tell you that evil is winning."
— *The Knight Industries Two Thousand,
a talking car affectionately known as K.I.T.T.*

When I was in kindergarten, in the 1980s, there were a couple of shows about technology that were extremely popular. One of them was on CBS in prime time, and it was called Airwolf.

In a typical episode of Airwolf, one-dimensional character actors playing criminals were about to get away with something, usually financial or mercenary in nature, and at the thrilling climax, as the theme song played, Stringfellow Hawke would jump in his amazing helicopter and use technology to track down the bad guys and unalive them with a large explosion, enough slow motion sparks to embarrass an angle grinder, and a column of smoke. It was repetitive, but exciting. The first few times.

There was also another show, on NBC, in which a pre-botox David Hasselhoff would drive around in a talking Pontiac while using technology to directly and pragmatically help people with their relatable human problems. The shows had some of the same ingredients. The car could transform into a turbine powered AI marvel capable of traveling three hundred miles per hour while carrying on a pleasant conversation in a voice that I realized later sounded suspiciously like Mr. Feeney from Boy Meets World.

In a prototypical episode of Knight Rider, a little girl is waiting for a heart transplant, and the heart is stolen by terrorists. In the nick of time, Michael Knight, aided by the most powerful and best-looking computer in the world, recovers the missing heart, and drives 300mph to get it to the medical team, just in time to save the little girl's life. The episode ends with the little girl, fresh scars on her chest, having a poignant conversation with the automobile. The thesis of the show was that with technology, even one person can make an outsized mark on the world.

Sometimes the last thing standing between evil desires and evil events is just one determined person. In other words, perhaps technology isn't just a dramatic event where bad things explode for our amusement, but perhaps it's a process — a tool that amplifies our efforts, a lever and fulcrum, and it can be used for good or evil or preparing your taxes. A recurring theme of the show is the great evil that is possible when technology is in the hands of bad people. To this day, few things make me as angry as a cyberattack on a hospital.

This show formed the way I think about technology. Technology is a force multiplier, and we have a moral obligation to figure out what it is for, and use it to its potential. As sticky Popsicle juice dribbled down my chin, I would mouth the words "one man can make a difference" as

Wilton Knight said them to Michael Knight, until somewhere along the line this idea got burned into my soul. It became important to me to help people use technology to make a difference in the world, just like Hasselhoff and his talking car.

The symbolism wasn't lost on me when David Hasselhoff hung from a crane and sang his original song *Looking For Freedom* at the Brandenburg gate as the Berlin wall crumbled around him in 1989. The Germans are perhaps the only people in the world who are more fanatical fans of Knight Rider than I am, because the actor who played Michael Knight was there with them in that moment, rejoicing over them with singing as east and west Germans became one nation again, protesting injustice, struggling with them for a better tomorrow for their children, tearing down the wall that attempted to separate them. I think Knight Rider is still syndicated in Germany.

My dad had a Pontiac Firebird that looked a lot like that car. I have wonderful memories of riding in the back seat, listening to Vangelis' Chariots of Fire, and feeling incredibly safe, because it looked like KITT. Fun bit of trivia - the distinctive red "scanner" on the front of the car was Glen Larson's idea. He was the producer of the show, and it was a callback to a show he produced a few years before called Battlestar Galactica, in which evil robots nearly conquer mankind.

In the 2014 Super Bowl commercial "Empowering Us All," McCann Erickson on behalf of Microsoft establishes the scene with a shot of a boy—a young kid with prosthetic legs—standing on a quiet suburban street. He's adjusting his prosthetics with a mix of concentration and determination, and there's something in his stance that tells you he's already learned to live with more grit than most of us ever will. "They told me I'd never walk," he says, his voice steady, defiant.

"What is technology?" a robotic-sounding voice asks. A moment later you realize that the narrator is a human with ALS who can't speak. Technology is among other things, his voice.

As the scene shifts, we meet others: a teacher with cerebral palsy who stands in front of her classroom, using a Microsoft Surface tablet to guide her students through a lesson. The classroom buzzes with energy, and you can see that her passion for teaching isn't just intact; it's thriving. We're taken to a rural clinic, where a doctor consults with a specialist thousands of miles away, using Microsoft Skype to bring the kind of expertise that might otherwise be out of reach. A woman turns on her cochlear implant for the first time, laughing and covering her mouth while tears stream down her cheeks.

And mine. Every damn time. Because when I watch that brilliant commercial I am smacked in the face with the importance and gravity of my inescapable purpose. We must use technology to move information to help people. This was the tagline for my company and I think about this idea every day. So many technically gifted people seem to get this exactly backwards. Because they watched Airwolf instead of Knight Rider, perhaps.

Technology is not reducible to a series of zeros and ones, sleek devices, talking cars, badass helicopters, blinking lights or SQL queries. It's something so much more visceral. At its best, when we use it properly, it bridges the chasm between what we hope is possible and what we are really capable of doing.

And there's that kid again, walking on a balance beam, then running on the track, his prosthetics propelling him forward. He's not just running; he's flying. The camera catches him in slow motion as he crosses the finish line, and for a second, everything else fades away and you forget the technology is there. You don't see the prosthetics anymore; you just see a boy, victorious, relishing in an impossible moment.

Technology isn't about devices; it's about what those devices make possible. It teaches us that maybe, just maybe, the future really is something we can shape, and that the tools to do it are already in our hands. As Knight Rider taught me, technology in the right hands can be a tool to "champion the cause of the innocent, the helpless, the powerless, in a world of criminals who operate above the law." So we have to get it into the right hands.

The computers have always been a means to an end. We must use technology to move information to help people.

3

CALIFORNIA

"Welcome to California: a land of dreams, but dreams are dangerous commodities; they usually require an extra large maintenance contract."
— *Brandon Walsh, Beverly Hills 90210*

I was born in Orange, California, but before I turned 3, my dad got transferred to Phoenix. Our last name, Phinney, (If you say it fin-knee, you're one of the good ones and I like you.) is frequently mispronounced. I recall one time we were checking into a hotel, and the clerk kept saying things like "Thank you for staying with us Mr. Puhinney. Did you have pleasant travels today, Mr. Puhinney? Will you be needing a wake up call Mr. Puhinney? And where are you coming in from today, Mr. Puhinney?"

My dad looked him dead in the eye and said "Puheenix."

I remember when I was about 8 or 9, there was a television commercial for "Real California Oranges." "Insist on the best," the announcer said. "Insist on Real California

Oranges." And when we would go to Basha's or Fry's or Alpha Beta, there would be a huge sign in the produce section that said "Real California Oranges."

So among the things I was excited about when I found out that I would be visiting my grandparents in California was getting my hands on a fresh Real California Orange. We flew into Burbank, and my parents dropped me off, probably preferring each other's exclusive company to mine for some wedding anniversary related reason, and I was delighted when a couple days later my grandma pulled into the parking lot at Ralph's Grocery in Pasadena. "Finally," I thought. "Real California Oranges!"

So we walked into the store, and I headed straight for the produce. And my heart sank when I saw it. Proudly hanging above a display of fresh and fragrant citrus was a sign that said "Real Florida Oranges." I guess people think fruit tastes better if it comes from far away.

I was surprised and excited to learn when I was twelve that our family was moving back to California. Nearly everything I knew about California I learned from watching "Beverly Hills, 90210," an Aaron Spelling prime time soap opera about some kids from Minnesota who relocated to one of America's most expensive zip codes. I supposed that I would roll up the sleeves of my t-shirt and learn to like R.E.M. and that would be that. Neither of those things were popular with kids in California, as it turned out. Aaron Spelling was full of shit.

But in California I found boating, snowboarding, bodyboarding, mountain biking, golf, and many other enjoyable outdoor activities. In Arizona, people stayed indoors for a good part of the year, but California was a perennial playground with a Mediterranean climate, postcard-worthy beaches, and incredible mountain vistas.

A friend of mine is planning his first visit to California and asked me sincerely if it was difficult to avoid the dangerous unhoused population and all the wildfires. In Texas, I recall that someone paid to put up a billboard that addressed Californians, imploring them to "please continue on I-40 until you have left our GREAT STATE OF TEXAS." During Covid, I guess a lot of us moved to areas that were inexpensive and unintentionally made them more expensive. When I visited Nashville, I saw people wearing t-shirts that said "Don't California my Tennessee." The President of the United States later blamed Californians for our wildfires, stating that we failed to rake our (federally managed) forests and that we caused our own drought by "dumping all the rainwater in the ocean."

There's a lot of hate for California out there, despite The Beach Boys and 2Pac and Katy Perry's commendable efforts at public relations.

Cable news, at the mention of California (or anywhere on the west coast), seems to cut to the same stock footage of a dumpster on fire. There's reasons my friend is afraid to visit, I just don't think those reasons are grounded in reality.

Despite the fear that has been carefully cultivated about Californians, if California were a country, it would be the fifth largest economy in the world. Our GDP is larger than what remains of the British Empire. California is one of a handful of "donor states" that consistently contributes billions more to the Federal budget than it receives in Federal funding. Hewlett-Packard, Apple, Intel, Meta/Facebook, Alphabet/Google, Fluor, Paypal, Chevron, Netflix, Tesla, Oracle, Disney, Cisco, Salesforce, eBay, Uber, Qualcomm, and so many other incredible American businesses got their start in the Golden State. Maybe it's not a coincidence that I started a business in California and it made me rich.

Yes, it's expensive here. But it's also incredibly beautiful. Once I was driving in the midwest, and remarked to my mother that there must be a large fire nearby because there was a crazy amount of ash falling from the sky. Then it occurred to me that the road was wet. Because it was snowing. Truthfully, most of us don't know how to shovel a sidewalk or scrape ice off of a windshield. I've wondered out loud what car covers are for. I took my family boating in the ocean on Christmas Day, and we saw dolphins swim up alongside our boat. I've been snowboarding and surfing on the same day. California isn't the apocalyptic dystopia that everyone says it is. It's ridiculously nice here, almost all the time.

More importantly to my story, California sees the lowest business failure rate for any state in America. Just 18.5% of California's businesses fail in the first year, so even though we started a business during a recession, we might have picked a good place to do it. Nationally, the average is about 25%, and in Washington State, you've only got a 59% chance of making it to your 13th month.

As business picked up, I would get pulled into service calls. One day I realized that I had 7 service calls, and all of them were within yards of SNA, known locally as John Wayne International Airport. Frequently I spent the entire day circling the airport, and realized that there is some correlation between access to jets and commerce.

I still think airport advertising is a great way to reach business owners.

I also recall that the Fortune 500 job where I started my career went away largely because local officials were persuaded to kill plans to build a better international airport. And John Wayne, which is still in place, remains one of the most dangerous airports in the country, partially because of its comically short runways, and partially because of its asinine requirement that pilots take off at full throttle, then reduce throttle after takeoff to reduce noise. Microphones record the sound pressure levels of passing jets and levy fines at airlines that fail to follow this dangerous procedure.

So, California has lots of airports, but why is it such a unique place to start and grow a business? Yes, it has the largest state economy of any U.S. State. That has to be a factor. Californians also enjoy excellent access to capital, particularly in Silicon Valley. It's a globally recognized hub of innovation and technology, and there are extensive networking and support organizations that assist small businesses with mentorship, funding, and resources. Author Daniel Lyons described Silicon Valley as "the American dream on steroids and Red Bull."

One organization that helped me immensely in those early years was SoCal BNI. BNI is an organization that I had done some web development work for prior to starting a business. Its founder, Dr. Ivan Misner, wrote several bestselling books, including a book called the 29% Solution, which debunks the popular myth of 6 degrees of separation, but arrives at the conclusion that the myth is true for 29% of the population. The book goes on to describe how to be in that 29%. In BNI, you stand up every week and talk about your business, until it becomes muscle memory, and you are encouraged to take meetings with other members during the week to strategize for mutual growth.

I helped start a new chapter, and was first an "education coordinator" and then a vice president, and eventually a director of several chapters. It's ironic that I was leading training seminars for other business owners before I considered my own business to be successful, but my first six figure deal was a BNI referral.

That's a story worth mentioning, come to think of it. In fact, for a while one of the success stories that they told people to convince them to join BNI was my story:

Late in the afternoon, I received a phone call from another BNI member. She told me she was asking for a favor and that it wasn't a real referral. She was a paralegal, and wanted me to reach out to a consulting CPA that she knew who had a computer question.

I thanked her and put off making the call. At the end of the day I took a deep breath and dialed the number.

The CPA was nice enough. He explained that he had a client who had experienced some data loss, and that as a result her business was struggling. He asked if I would go meet with his client in Los Angeles.

I said I would, and he copied me on an email introduction. I wasn't very busy, but it would take me almost an hour to drive to the appointment and another hour to drive home. I was early, and stopped for a coffee near their office. Out of curiosity or boredom, I plugged her name into a search engine, and learned that she was the winner of the sixth largest lottery jackpot in California's history. 96 million dollars.

I vowed to myself at that moment that I would never take advantage of her, and would treat her like any other prospective customer, but my posture involuntarily straightened.

Our lottery winner turned out to be a genuine and kind and down to earth lady who had always wanted to be an entrepreneur. Before she won the lottery, she lived in a motel and worked in a factory that manufactured sulfuric acid. She was exactly the sort of person that you'd hope might win the lottery. Sadly, someone she had trusted had allegedly been engaging in fraud, and once she realized she was probably a victim, she and her partner asked me "how can we prevent this from happening again?"

So I showed her our service catalog and explained how everything worked. She asked for quotes on literally every service we offered, and then signed a multi-year agreement for all of them. Then she asked us to do it again for another company she had acquired on the east coast, then for another company they later acquired in California.

Truthfully, I spent most of my time with them trying to talk them out of spending more money on IT services and equipment, but that referral gave us a running start we desperately needed, and as a result, I became much more bold when asking for referrals.

I understand some of the reasons people don't like California, but I can't relate to them. Things like that just seem to happen in California more than they happen in other places. If just 29% of the world is really separated by six degrees of networking like Dr. Misner says, I bet a disproportionate quantity of those 29 percenters have spent time in the Golden State.

So the deck might have been stacked a little in my favor, just because of where I was born and where my parents decided to live. I'm trying not to be one of those guys who is born on third base and brags about hitting a triple. But I was born in California, and it's where I'm from, and I'm not ashamed of that. I hope you're proud of where you came from, too.

4

DABBAWALAS

"We are carrying food from someone's home to their loved ones. That is a huge responsibility, and we take it very seriously."
— Subhash Talekar, Dabbawala

I visited India once. A place of striking contrasts and thousands of years of incredible history. One of those places that changes the way you think about the world and your place in it. Driving in India is something else. In America, you're responsible for your blind spots. In India, drivers fold in their mirrors, to save space, because lanes are ignored, and because you're only responsible for what you can see through your windshield. If you want to merge, you just signal, honk, and start moving over. The person next to you needs to either manage to get ahead of you or hit the brakes.

It was humbling touring the India Institute of Technology and then walking the streets of Gurgaon, a New Delhi suburb. In Gurgaon, bright young people with advanced degrees proudly carry briefcases to and from their jobs in mid-rise buildings for Dell, Microsoft, and other Fortune 500 companies. Their income supports their extended families, often pays for a cook and a maid, and allows them to invest in real estate.

I was told that most of these people work in call centers. I imagine them spending their days being talked down to by Americans who assume incorrectly that anyone with an accent must also be an idiot. If that weren't bad enough, they're often subjected to the indignity of adopting absurdly Western names like "Craig." I suppose it's meant to make things easier, but I feel like they might as well tell me their name is Santa Claus or Kermit the frog, if only to add an extra layer of absurdity to an already ridiculous situation for both of us.

But that day I saw in their eyes intelligence, dignity, and purpose, and for the first time, I found myself admiring Indian call center workers.

870 miles away in Mumbai, there's a fascinating segment of India's workforce that has captured the attention of business leaders and scholars from institutions like FedEx, MIT, London Business School, Harvard, McKinsey, and Deloitte. These are the Dabbawalas—workers whose name, in Hindi, translates to something like "lunchbox carrier." On the surface, their task might seem simple: delivering home-cooked lunches in stackable tin containers to workers across Mumbai and then collecting the empties before the day is done. But the real story here is their precision and reliability. They operate with a level of efficiency that rivals

the most advanced logistical systems in the world. Almost no mistakes. But beyond the mechanics, what's truly remarkable is the pride they take in their work. The Dabbawalas are not just lunch carriers—they are integral to the city's ecosystem. Their sense of purpose and self-esteem, rooted in tradition and service, is palpable and contagious.

I've watched several documentaries where Dabbawalas are interviewed, and I've observed that they universally seem to think they have the best job in the world. They're incredibly proud of the work they do. The city of Mumbai even honored them with a giant statue of a bronze Dabbawala. They use a cryptic system of symbols and exchanges to get the food where it goes. Many of them are illiterate. The only education many of them receive is in how to be a Dabbawala. They earn approximately $150/month in US dollars at time of writing. They succeed consistently against incredible odds because they believe– no, that's not right. They absolutely know that their work is important. "Without food, people can't accomplish anything," one Dabbawala explained. Without the advantages of modern technology, they give their hard working customers a delicious taste of home every day, over 200,000 times a day, before the curry has a chance to cool off.

An acquaintance of mine was an early hire at a Canadian IT Managed Service Provider where they had an aggressive medieval-themed brand. Famously, the technicians would get the company logo tattooed on their chest, branded right where it would be if they were wearing the company polo, so that if they took off their work shirts, the logo would still be there, on their bare chests, in the same spot. According to rumor, the CEO would, on their five year anniversary with the company, send them on an all expense paid trip to Vegas on the condition that they return with the tattoo. I'm not sure how they got this through HR, but I thought it was amazing that in this day and age, people would love their company and colleagues so much that they would want to commit to wearing that polo shirt forever.

That company was later acquired by a very well known copier company.

When I first met this fellow at a conference, I asked him if he had to get a tattoo of the copier company's logo. He laughed loudly for a moment, and then his face went serious and he told me it wasn't funny. He refused to tell me if he had the tattoo or not. I hope they can change that old logo into a cool skull for him or something.

I enjoy trying to help people understand the importance of their jobs. Once, I was walking through a warehouse with a woman who was a key player in operations for a customer of ours that distributed rubber O rings. As we walked, she made a sarcastic comment that suggested she felt that her job was trivial.

I said, "Stop what you're doing and listen to me for a minute."

She did. I had her full attention.

I told her that when I was a little kid, I used to go to Burger King every week, and in the middle of the restaurant they had a huge rotating scale model of the Challenger space shuttle, and that I liked to sit next to it and watch it slowly twirl while I ate my Whopper. One day I went there with my dad and the entire model space shuttle was covered in black cloth.

It had become a memorial, and it was adorned with scotch taped crayon drawings of space shuttles and grinning stick figure astronauts contributed by students from a nearby elementary school. Cellophane-wrapped flowers had been placed at the base of the model. No one sat next to it that day, and they later removed it entirely, because the Challenger shuttle exploded above Cape Canaveral, Florida on January 28th, 1986. Among the seven dead astronauts was Christa McAuiliffe, a high school social studies teacher from New Hampshire who had won a contest, a mother of two who was legendary for her homemade chocolate chip cookies.

Schoolchildren and their teachers watched the launch live on television in horror, as CNN's Tom Mintier said, "Obviously something is wrong. We have a- a problem with the vehicle. At about a minute and 15 seconds after liftoff, a plume of smoke, flame, and then a large fireball erupted."

"Do you know why that shuttle with those brave, bright-eyed astronauts on board tragically exploded that day?" I asked.

She had no idea.

"Someone put the wrong rubber O ring in it," I explained, "and rocket fuel went somewhere it wasn't supposed to go. The fuel ignited so all of the astronauts died in a violent explosion on national television." I looked over at a nearby shelf where a box said "Northrop Grumman" on it. I gestured toward it with my chin and said, "Do you know what Northrop Grumman does?" She didn't.

"Among other things, they make rocket boosters for NASA."

Her eyes steeled and her expression hardened with fresh resolve. She thanked me and went back to work. She was a top producer there for years.

I had a similar conversation with a land buyer for a homebuilder we worked with. I said to him, "What could possibly be more important than making space for families to connect? How many of people's best memories are going to exist in the spaces you create with this land?" He said he'd never thought about it that way. I told him he should absolutely think about it that way.

I once met James Genus, who plays bass for Herbie Hancock, and also for as long as I can remember, in the Saturday Night Live house band. After a canceled flight, I found myself wandering around Manhattan in the middle of the night, cursing JetBlue under my breath and looking for contact lens solution. It was shortly after things had begun reopening after Covid, when we learned to live without minor conveniences like clear vision, and although I didn't find an open drug store, I did find an open bar.

Exhausted and thirsty, I walked inside and sat down at the end of the bar. A fellow walked in behind me and sat down next to me, and he immediately looked incredibly familiar to me, like I'd seen him a hundred times, but I couldn't quite place him. I might never have figured it out, but he was wearing a Broadway Video shirt, and for some reason I recognized that as the name of Lorne Michaels' production company. I asked him if he played bass. Surprised, he said yes. Then I asked him if he played bass in the Saturday Night Live band.

"Are you going to make this weird?" he said.

"I'll try not to, but I think that's awesome," I told him. "Can I buy your next round?"

He relaxed a little.

A few minutes later, we were talking like old friends, discussing the mounting conflict in Ukraine and the show's writers over the years, and some of his favorite musical guests, and he said something self-effacing. It was happening again.

I said, "Do you know how important you are to that show?"

He stared at me and blinked.

I said, "James, they always cut to you in the opening monologue. Do you know why they do that?"

He shook his head.

"Because you laugh at every damn joke, man."

He laughed. That big soulful infectious laugh.

"And that's incredibly important, not just to the show, but to America, because no matter what happened this week and what happens next week, no matter how scary or sad it is, no matter how anxious it makes us, we know you're going to be there doing your thing, reminding us that it's still ok to laugh."

He joked that he was going to ask Lorne for a raise. I hope he got it. He deserves one. I meant everything I said.

In our business, we put up propaganda posters around the office about the things our customers were doing with technology. Our customers flew jets and built them. They designed and built houses, air conditioned the shops on Main Street at Disneyland, and picked up people in developing countries off of the ground and put them in brand new wheelchairs. They administered mentoring programs for children, provided food support to unhoused kids, and supplied sealing O rings that were used for transferring all kinds of fluids, from peanut oil to rocket fuel. Our customers did amazing things, and we used technology to move information to help them. I learned this from the Dabbawalas. We spend more time with the people we work with than we do with our partners and children. If people understand a bit of what it all means, they become more than just hired hands. In my experience, a little bit of vision and a lot of respect can increase productivity tenfold.

One moment I'll always remember — when we were about to be acquired, the buyers asked if they could visit our office, posing as potential customers. My family and I spent the entire weekend tidying up the office before they walked in on Monday. Every cable was wrapped. Every piece of hardware was boxed or binned or stacked. I met them in the lobby, and after a few minutes of conversation in the conference room, we took a restroom break. Before we reconvened, I realized the buyers were walking through the office, reading every word on every poster. I'd like to think that they were thinking about what would be on their posters, the people they had helped. What their team had accomplished up to that point, and what we would be able to do together.

The narrative that I'd positioned to inspire our staff had accrued real monetary value in the business we were about to sell.

We had a key person leave the business somewhere around 2018, and he left a big hole. Our staff and our customers were concerned about the impact to the business from this departure. So was I. I gathered the team in the conference room and summarily promoted everyone. Just updated the org chart and explained how each person was now a leader, accountable for part of operations. It was the best idea I had at the time. It really worked. I put my trust in our people, and everyone stepped up.

Gino Wickman has written several excellent business books, and is responsible for creating "Traction," an entrepreneurial operating system and a better way to run meetings. He likens problems and challenges in business to "monkeys" and encourages managers to not allow personnel to leave their monkeys in the manager's office.

While my instincts have sometimes lead away from this posture, I have learned that a necessary ingredient for scale and success is to empower your people to solve problems independently, which means you need to continuously remind staff that you trust them, that it is ok to make mistakes as long as you learn from them, and that you've trained and empowered them well to make high quality decisions on behalf of the company. When it's clear that their decisions and input are not just valued, but are instrumental, and they believe that the power to fix problems is well within their grasp, your best people will start to exhibit leadership, which means you will spend less time rounding up their monkeys, as the entire organization will be able to execute with more alacrity and accomplish more than one important thing at a time.

In addition to deputizing people to make decisions, I realized that there were some key tasks that I needed to require everyone in the company to be able to do. One of my "first day goals" for each employee was that they knew how to answer the phone and create a ticket in our PSA software. If things went seriously sideways and we received hundreds of calls at the same time, which happened once or twice in ten years, I wanted everyone to feel comfortable and competent to talk to customers and document their service requests for later follow-up. All of our technicians learned how to program and install our firewall, build and configure a phone system, and set up backup and endpoint security and our management agent on an endpoint. Importantly, they all were trained to do things the same way.

When they train bank tellers, they want them handling real money, all the time, so that when they hold a bill that's counterfeit, they will instinctively know that it feels wrong. Keeping deployments uniform yielded similar benefits to us. Everyone knew that the standard configuration worked, so troubleshooting became about spotting variables. What's different about *this* setup from every other customer that's operating well?

I took an economics class in high school. The teacher, Coach Roberts, who also taught golf, had two clearly articulated goals for all of his students. He wanted us to be comfortable filing our own tax returns, and he wanted us to memorize the definition of "gross national product," which he made us repeat in unison thirty times in a row, a couple times a week. Gross national product is "the total value of all final goods and services measured by the prices paid for them in a year." I'll never forget that.

Similarly, in our business there were a few things that everyone was expected to know. We came up with the acronym "BEARS" which we used to help everyone remember Backup, Endpoint security, remote Access, Remote maintenance (patch management), and Spam filtering. If I asked "what services do we manage?" everyone would rattle off that response. Technicians and managers soon turned it into a verb, and would say things like "there's a new laptop for Mr. Washington at Alpha Escrow on the test bench. Do you know if anyone has BEARSed it yet? I'd like to get it out to him today."

I occasionally asked other IT Managed Service Providers what services they are managing, and usually the answer was that "it's a little different for everyone." One of the secrets of our success? Our answer was the same for everyone, at least as similar as we could possibly manage.

We did performance reviews once a year. Personnel would complete a self-evaluation and then I reviewed it with them and their supervisor. On one occasion, I sat across the table from someone during a scheduled review. My mind wandered as I was casually discussing some upcoming challenges, when I was interrupted by a small voice that cracked when it nervously asked me, "Can you please skip to the part of this where you tell me how I'm doing?"

I quickly filled out the review form on the spot, and gave that person a perfect review. I hoped we could get back to discussing business. Then the tears came. That validation was so powerful for that person. And it was so easy for me to sincerely give.

It seems like employers have way too much power, and I was reminded of that on that day. Why on earth should it be up to me whether or not someone can see a doctor? I imagine that insurers gave employers that power in the first place because if you have to have a job to get insurance, people who are too sick to work will fall off of the actuarial table.

It's an incredible privilege to get to pick the people you work with, and I have to say I picked some really good people. Furthermore, some of my best hires were people who weren't obvious choices. I hired a butcher, a paramedic, a web developer, and several military veterans into technical support and engineering roles, for example. I learned that people who had worked for Disney were usually very good at customer service, and I watched a copier repairman grow into someone all of the technicians looked up to, and then I made him their supervisor. Today he works for Microsoft. I'm sure he would have been successful with or without me, but I can't help but feel proud of him.

I loved walking through our parking lot, because every year it seemed like our staff had slightly nicer cars. Even as my own car at the time, a 2008 Ford Taurus X, wouldn't have turned many heads, there would be much better cars in my future.

One of my favorite things that I got to do was hosting the annual holiday party, where I would talk about each person's achievements and talent to an audience of their significant others and their peers, stressing their importance to the mission of our business and our customers, noting their responsibilities, their skills, and the things I admired about them, then I'd hand them an envelope with a check in it, and I did my best every year to make sure the check had a comma in the total. As we grew, it became more expensive to do that, but it was so much fun.

Employment is first and foremost an exchange of value, and I've learned that taking care of people financially is a valid way to motivate them, but people also love to understand their place in the story, and they deserve to receive respect. If you are a people leader, and you're not making the most of those opportunities to enrich your people, I recommend that you evaluate why you aren't, because attrition is expensive.

5

RIDING THE JET SKI

"Small is beautiful when small is skilled, flexible, and efficient, while big is clumsy, slow, and unwieldy."
— E.F. Schumacher

Picture an aircraft carrier. Go ahead, really conjure it up—the enormity of it, the massive gray hulk cutting through the ocean. Now, think about how many people it takes to make that thing go. Not just move, but operate, in the fullest sense of the word. Think of the sheer human will and horsepower involved in getting that monstrosity to change directions when it's at full throttle. The physics involved in that request must be like asking a glacier to pivot.

You've got a determined crew—brave, gritty, maybe a little bit tired after months at sea—turning dials, monitoring oil pressure, keeping one eye on the gauges and the other on the horizon. These aren't seafaring automatons. They're people. They've got stories, quirks, breakfast preferences. And here they are, unified in this mind-boggling task of steering their floating city through the darkness of night without running it aground.

An operating aircraft carrier is a breathtaking sight to behold. I've seen one. Well, sort of. I've been aboard the

U.S.S. Midway, which is, okay, retired. It's permanently parked in San Diego now, a leviathan that's been turned into a floating museum. It's like a giant relic from a war movie, except it's real and you can climb around on it. If you're ever in the area, it's worth a couple hours of your time. Wander around, let the scale of it mess with your head. You'll get a sense—just a fraction—of what it took to take that beast out to sea, to set it in motion, to keep it from barreling into a peninsula.

As a cybersecurity professional and a member of Infragard, an information sharing partnership between FBI, DHS, CISA, and the private sector, I have access to some limited national security information, and once accepted an invitation to attend an online briefing about the conflict in Ukraine which was quickly escalating into war. The summary of it was that Ukraine had a better shot at defending itself than anyone was giving it credit for, because the Russian military was terrible at logistics. The consultant leading the talk essentially predicted that Russian tanks would run out of gas, because they didn't have fueling infrastructure in place, that they would need to loot homes and shops for food, because there was no long term plan to feed them, and that unless Kiev toppled in 72 hours, they would struggle to find suitable places to land air infrastructure, and might become reliant on easily interruptible rail systems for supply.

The American Military, in contrast, is extremely skilled at logistics, and can land not just a fighting force, but all the supplies to occupy land indefinitely, anywhere in the world, in a matter of hours, due to careful planning, skill, and capability.

Aircraft carriers are part of that system, and there is a reason why we spend tax dollars to build them. But there are some disadvantages to these floating cities. Specifically, they are not very maneuverable.

I remember a trip to Lake Mojave when I was a much younger man. 22 years ago, I was strong, and thin, and I had great hair. My girlfriend, who is now my wife, and I and a couple of our friends had joined my future in-laws and some of their friends to camp along the banks of the Colorado river, and they brought a couple boats and some Sea-Doo waverunners, which are personal watercraft like Jet Skis but are designed to be ridden from a seated position. The boats carried our camping gear and food, but everyone enjoyed a turn on the waverunners.

When it was our turn, Kelly wrapped her arms around me and held on tight. At some point, I noticed a peculiar and welcome phenomenon: the faster I went, and the quicker I turned, the tighter her grip around me became, until I could feel her breath on my neck, hot and close, and the feeling of my own heart beating faster from adrenaline and attraction. Naturally, I pushed the limits. We tore through the coves along the bank of the river, skimming across the water and testing the laws of physics. I turned sharper, faster, as the world was reduced to just the two of us and the spray of water behind. I sought and found the limits of her grip until gravity, centrifugal force, and hubris caught up to us, and we were thrown from the watercraft, bobbing like corks in ugly neon life jackets, sharing a passionate kiss under the Nevada sun as she pretended to be angry with me. For a moment, time stood still.

You might imagine that McDonald's, the ubiquitous titan of fast food and franchising, built its empire on burgers—but it's more than that. It's the real estate, the sheer volume of it, the ability to sell you a meal and own the land under your feet while you eat it at over 40,000 locations worldwide. They're always tinkering with their menu, rolling out seasonal novelties like the McRib and the Shamrock Shake, or salty failures like the McPizza and Arch Deluxe. If you don't remember those, it's okay. Almost no one does.

Meanwhile, In-N-Out has quietly perfected the cheeseburger. They serve up a simple, flawless creation at a price that feels revolutionary in an era of $15 artisanal craft brioche nonsense. And here's the thing—they rarely touch their menu. Sure, they have that "secret menu," but that has to be one of the worst kept secrets in the western United States.

McDonalds purchases its beef from nationally recognizable distributors while In-N-Out owns and closely manages their entire supply chain from the cows to the stockyards, to the bakeries, to the refrigerator trucks that deliver to the company owned restaurants. In-N-Out doesn't franchise. The whole enterprise is family owned.

There are advantages to scale and also advantages to agility. If you are small, you can change directions quickly, fail fast, and recover faster. You can give your customers a level of personal attention that a larger entity will struggle to match.

One thing that amused me over the years was how small businesses wanted to look big and large businesses wanted to look small.

For example, when our entire team was about five people, we had this really corporate sounding telephone system with menus and prompts like "press 3 for technical support or 4 for billing" to give people the impression that we were formidable. When our team was three times that size and we were juggling hundreds of accounts, we programmed the phone system to recognize the caller and route them to someone who knew their account, and hired dedicated customer service personnel, just so that we could answer the phone and say, "Hello Barry, how are you today?" It became a challenge to hang on to the strengths of being small as we started to adjust to being a bit bigger. Later on when I was CIO of a company that had a team of over a thousand people and was profiled in the Wall Street Journal, our customer service representatives and salespeople would routinely give out their direct numbers to clients and prospects.

Here's what I'm getting at: Be who you are. If you're on a Jet Ski, dash in and out of the coves, intentionally throw yourself off the watercraft, and kiss the girl. If you're In-N-Out, lean into the advantage you have by being smaller— quality control— and be careful about introducing too many ideas too fast, because McDonalds can afford to risk a million dollars on a bad decision, but when there are three things on the menu, they better all be good. If you're a small business, you already have advantages that your larger competitors covet. Lean into that. Stop pretending you're gigantic. Embrace being small.

We lost an account one time. It was a local nonprofit that I was emotionally attached to, because of their wonderful mission and great staff, and we were giving them a big discount and doing a fairly good job by my estimation, but someone from a bigger MSP joined their advisory board, and he wanted the organization to be a case study for his company.

So, we scheduled a call to discuss the transition with the new provider who was taking over the account, and I realized that at this stage of our growth, both of us were listed in the CRN MSP 500, a list of the top 500 IT service providers in North America. Both of us were in the same town, and we were doing pretty much the same business. When their account manager and I joined the conference bridge, we were joined by 13 people from the other company and one representative from the customer. There were 16 of us on the call.

We were reasonably well prepared for what they were going to ask, because we were usually on the other end of a transition between providers, but this call took forever because each person on the call wanted to sound like they were important and knowledgeable. I joked in a private message to my only ally on the call that we should post the dial in info on slack and invite every single person we worked with to join the call and introduce themselves. As I wrote that, I realized something. If you total up the payroll cost of all of the people on that call, our company was spending, perhaps a few hundred dollars. But our competitor was spending thousands, especially if everyone had a couple of action items to follow up on afterwards. Maybe the client was impressed, but if it takes that many people to drive the boat, that boat is going to need a whole lot of gas at some point. If they matched or beat our pricing, they probably lost a lot of money on that account.

A small business has a kind of freedom that large companies stare at wistfully. They are nimble, able to jump on new trends or abandon old ones, and can change direction as fast as a caffeinated squirrel. But the game isn't just about speed. It's about intimacy. While large businesses lumber around like dinosaurs at a skate park, they'll spend millions conducting A-B research on the optimal way to innovate while the small business down the street is already two months deep into a quirky new product line that no one saw coming. You know that feeling of putting a record on, that slight scratchy warmth before the music starts? Big businesses try hard to cultivate that kind of analog authenticity, but small businesses create without much effort. They are rough around the edges, which is precisely where charm lives.

Consider the kind of space a small business inhabits in your mind. You don't have a relationship with Starbucks; you have a transaction with them. But at a small coffee shop they remember how you take your latte. When you're running late for work, they make it in advance without you even asking. Small businesses can be personal in a way that large businesses have forgotten how to be. When you're small, you are interested in today—this moment—right now—and that can make all the difference if you let it.

Most people, if asked to talk about the strength of the American economy, might be tempted to talk about the Fortune 500. Apple, Google, Tesla, Nvidia. These companies are great success stories, and I certainly admire them. But there are 334 million people in America. How many of them work at a Fortune 500 company? I looked it up for you. About 29.2 million. So, that's, what, about nine percent? Where does everyone work then?

According to the United States Small Business Administration, there are 33.3 million small businesses in America, defined as companies with 500 or fewer employees, which is greater than 99% of the total number of businesses in this country. These companies collectively employ 61.6 million people, more than twice as many as the Fortune 500, and about 46% of the total workforce in the United States. Small businesses are putting food on a lot of families' tables and are perhaps the most important economic engines in America. They do this with minimal capital requirements, and usually without slick ad campaigns or government funding.

In the worst moments of the pandemic, The CARES Act, the grand, sprawling, panic-stricken document that it was, did something unexpected—it placed its bets on small businesses. The daycares, the dry cleaners, the landscapers, the millions of micro-empires that seemed so fragile and yet, in truth, were the vertebrae of this country's economic spine. Without these businesses, there would be no spine. Without the spine, there would be no standing. And without standing, well, we'd just be a heap on the ground, wouldn't we? A disgusting boneless motionless blob of a country.

So Congress, in a fit of rare clarity, acted. It looked past the banks, past the multinational conglomerates, and said, "Let's give some money to the people who open the doors and turn on the lights." Suddenly, there was a spotlight on these essential businesses. Because small businesses are not just American, they are in a meaningful sense, America.

The CARES Act wasn't just about saving these businesses—it was about saving the owners, the employees, their suppliers, and delivery guys and customers. It was about recognizing that the local pizza spot is more than a place to grab a slice; it's also a hub of community, a lifeline for the adjunct college professor who needs a second job, for the kid quietly saving up to be one of his students, for the single mom trying to make rent. By directing funds to small businesses, Congress helped keep these delicate ecosystems alive.

Today, people spill a lot of ink about the relatively small percentage of fraudulent claims that were filed during that time, but the plan was surprisingly effective, even if it helped more people than Congress intended and resulted in considerable inflation. It did what a law rarely does—it actually worked when we needed it to. I want us to look back on this chapter of American history and let it remind us that the real economic giants of America were smaller than we thought. Because when small businesses got back on their feet, so did the rest of us.

6

THE PRICE IS RIGHT

"People don't like to be sold, but they love to buy."
— *Jeffrey Gitomer*

When I graduated from college, I had two things that every parent who has ever written a tuition check hopes their investment will achieve: a fiancée and a decent job. Like the video production interns who work for Saul Goodman in *Better Call Saul*, I had been making business videos for a gentleman I met at church, and after the dot com bubble burst, he helped me get an interview at an engineering and construction firm that had about 50,000 employees and a big presence in the local market. The family who started the company had recently donated a large decorative fountain to the university and put their family name on it. My mom made me stand next to it for a picture.

We had an enviable schedule with 9-hour work days and every other Friday off, and these incredibly complex time sheets to fill out in their ERP system, SAP. While I worked in marketing and all of my "clients" were other employees, I was expected, it was explained to me, to have "high utilization" which meant being "billable" all the time.

I was fortunate in that some of the best people in marketing liked me for some reason, and they not only taught me some stuff, but they also shared some projects with me, along with the coveted billing codes that allowed me to charge time to other departments. I managed to stay at about 85% billable most of the time, and they told me that I needed to reach 100%, which was just about impossible because it took me two hours just to fill out the time sheet, and we had mandatory trainings and meetings all the time.

Until something happened.

I'd been working for weeks on a presentation video for my friend's boss, who later ran the Oil and Gas division and became CEO of the company. A president of another division found out from a spy in my department that I was working on a video and it was pretty good. He asked me to make a video for him, too. So I worked for about 70 hours straight, and made him a very expensive video so that he wouldn't be upstaged at an internal company meeting. Not only did this get me past 100% utilization, but at some point I think I was 4x billable for every hour I worked, due to labor laws in California intended to disincentivize that sort of exploitation.

As I touched the limit of "billable hours" that were humanly possible, the thought occurred to me that if you bill by the hour–if you sell your time, you can't bill more than 24 hours in a day. You can't bill 25 hours unless you're lying or own a flux capacitor.

Later, when we started hiring employees, I found myself talking about billable hours and utilization, but from the other side of the table. I struggled to get our first employee to be 50% billable. Adding to my frustration, we had a growing mountain of vendors who expected to be paid on time every month, which meant I had to get out there and sell, get out there and bill hours, and make sure we collected some receivables.

When I first heard about managed services, I thought it was a scam. I figured providers would, instead of working hard for the customer all the time like I did, just put a few systems in place, apply some automation, and bill them a lot of money for doing not very much work.

Slowly, I realized that it was really a response to what the customers wanted, and that it would get us on the same side of the table. I never intentionally took advantage of anyone, but one time when I arrived at a service call, a customer looked at me and sardonically quipped, "What are you doing here? Is your boat payment due or something?"

In a managed services model, you and the customer work to decrease your utilization by improving your processes. You both bleed when there is downtime, so they know you're doing everything you can to avoid it, and when there is a problem, they know you're getting it fixed as fast as you can, because incentives are aligned - there's no reason to slow walk the solution if the bill is a static amount every month.

I tried to convince my partners that we should pivot, full steam ahead into this model. At the time, our pricing model was cribbed from cellular providers. Customers bought a block of hours at a discount that expired at the end of the month. Buying larger blocks got them a better discount. My partners were initially less than excited about this idea. It was a big change.

But then one of our flagship accounts, a nationally recognized brand, and probably the only one of those we had at the time, let us know that they were considering a move to another IT provider, specifically because they wanted managed services. Their salesperson had put his finger on something that annoyed them - unless they hit the exact number of hours that they had prepaid for, they would either have to pay for additional time, or they would have paid for time they didn't use. I asked them if they would consider staying with us, if we could deliver similar services and pricing to our competitor, and they said they would consider that.

So I escalated my messaging to my partners.

"This is a change or die moment for us," I told them. "We cannot lose this account, and they're right. The way we do this is dumb."

And to their credit, they committed to read the book *Managed Services in a Month* by Karl Palachuk and have a conversation about it. In this book, Karl explains what managed services is, how to sell it, how to price it, and why it's the right answer for IT providers and their customers. That book helped us save the account, and probably our business.

Instead of starting the month at zero or close to it,

wondering where I was going to find enough work to pay the bills, I could focus more of my attention on making things great for our customers. If they needed something, I didn't have to sell them on it, I could just do it, especially if it would save us all time in the long run. Instead of getting paid when things broke, we were incentivized to make sure they didn't break.

One of my favorite things about our new model was that many of the things we sold like firewalls were no longer optional - they just came with the service. Instead of selling time, we began selling outcomes. If the customer had no downtime, they would get more work done, and we would have fewer emergency service calls. We wanted the same thing - to engineer the system so well that we didn't have to do much to keep it running. It also flipped the script on utilization, because we started viewing labor as a cost and not a benefit.

Getting a proposal out was dead simple, too. I only needed a rough estimate of the number of sites, computers, and servers the customer had, and I could produce a quote with that. We wrote into the agreement that they would be billed for the actual number of devices, locations, and servers they had that month, so even if they grossly underestimated what they had during the discovery, we could right-size it once we had access to the environment.

The second customer that we transitioned to managed services was the first company that had ever written us a five figure check. I remember my hands shaking a little when I deposited it, and the three of us working late nights installing graphics cards, transferring files, and refreshing their desktop computers with faster replacements.

The President of the company was a Six Sigma black belt who had previously worked in management at GE and had been a division officer in the Navy, stationed on a nuclear-powered aircraft carrier. He ran his business with the discipline and intensity you would expect of a man who was accustomed to preparing to win a war. He valued precision, and would let you know when you made a mistake.

Once, when we were in the process of restoring some data from a backup, he asked me a question.

"Do you know what's significant about the figure $11,586.62?"

I didn't, but smelled a trap.

He went on to say, "That's how much it costs us for one hour of downtime, in payroll, in lost sales, in overhead that we can't recoup. Get us going 30 minutes faster, and you're saving us as much money as we paid you last month."

I started really thinking about that. It was motivational, which was what he intended. He strongly implied that he would spend more money to avoid an outcome where everyone had an unscheduled break. If we could prevent that kind of pain, we could not only justify a higher fee, but he showed me that we would have earned it. Soon, he signed a 3 year agreement and we were on the same side of the table, working toward a common goal: 100% uptime.

The next customer that converted was a homebuilder that seemed to grow by about 6 employees a month, consistently. The new pricing model meant that every time they ordered a new workstation, their monthly bill increased slightly, and they just built that cost into their expectations. Years later, that company was acquired by the largest publicly traded homebuilder in Japan.

Another time a customer taught me something important that stuck with me was a deal I lost. This chap needed a phone system for his business, and I was excited to work with him. He was a charismatic guy, I genuinely liked him, and wanted to do a great job. At the time, we were installing a custom phone system that was disruptively priced, and we would connect it to some basic Cisco handsets that we sourced from our distributor. The package was a good deal, but my customer didn't know or care how much a phone system cost.

He did, however, believe that he knew what a phone should cost.

I had lazily pushed the handsets through to the quote with the distributor's suggested retail price. Our cost on them was about $105, and the distributor's website said we should be selling them for $169.00 or something like that. He received my quote, and immediately went on Amazon.com to see if the price was fair, and found the same handsets for sale for $109.

He called me, hot out of the gate with flashes of anger

and annoyance in his tone, and while we were talking, he emailed me a screenshot of the Amazon listing, and then asked me point blank if I thought he was stupid. He implied that I was dishonest and predatory. It was a tough conversation, I became defensive, and I not only lost the sale, I lost the entire account.

What I should have said was that he had found a great price, and that I'd be happy to set up those phones if he wanted to get them himself from Amazon, and thanked him for telling me about it. Or I could have told him that the phones on Amazon are gray market and he might have issues if he tries to make a warranty claim, but that I would go through deal registration with Cisco and see if an additional discount was possible. I did not say those things. It caught me off guard. I totally choked.

I don't think he understood the value of what I was really offering, but that was my fault. He understood that he could get cheaper phones if he went around me, and that made him suspect that the things he didn't understand were probably similarly, from his perspective, overpriced. It wasn't his fault. The deal was overall fair, but I made a mistake. I failed to consider it from his perspective, and I didn't align the price with his expectations.

Years later, I had an epiphany about phones.

People had pretty much stopped using them, but they still wanted one on every desk for some reason. Smelling an opportunity, I started tracking how much people really used their office phones, and I figured out that on average, each phone handset was used for less than 500 minutes each month. This meant that instead of sourcing unlimited SIP trunks, we could pay by the minute and cover the cost of their calls for a per capita cost of a little over four bucks. Buying the airtime on demand from a SIP trunking provider also made the phones elastic, so instead of trying to guess how many "call paths" they needed to have active simultaneously, everyone could now be on the phone at the same time, which was perceived as a significant benefit.

I made the handsets free, I made the phone system free, I made the support free, and I started selling unlimited calling for $25/handset/month. And do you know what happened?

People thanked me for it. They thought it was very reasonable. They liked having a predictable cost, and not worrying that their call was costing the company money. I could also discount it by 30% if I wanted to, and still make a decent margin. Ultimately we made way more money, while the customers felt like they were stealing from us.

I made the thing they ascribe value to—the handsets—free. We were actually losing money on every new phone customer for the first couple months, but obviously that was a short term problem. I had moved the profit into a column that they didn't understand or care about, and I amortized their startup costs, which made them feel better about the entire thing. I started looking for more opportunities to do this.

Bundling became an important strategy for us. By the late 2010s, phishing attacks were everywhere, multiplying like rabbits on an apocalyptic mission to ruin us all. We responded by combining security awareness training and multi factor authentication into a bolt-on "security pack" and sold it at a significant markup.

Instead of positioning the tools like a bunch of spare parts, and billing by the hour, we became focused on offering end to end, comprehensive solutions to real business problems. Once it occurred to us that the whole is worth more than the sum of its parts, we found ourselves billing many multiples of our old hourly rates, creating a business that had value outside of its staff and owners. We unlocked the secret to predictable growing revenue for years to come and our customers signed evergreen contracts. Our balance sheet started to show that there was real value in what we had built, because we had finally stopped trying to sell our time.

Now there was no ceiling on what was possible.

And that's when I became certain that our plan would work. Someone would definitely want to buy the business that we were building, and for the first time, I started to really understand how the business could continue to thrive without my direct and constant effort. It was like discovering fire. We were no longer the plumbers of the digital world, showing up to fix a leak. We had crossed the Rubicon, and there was no turning back.

The Price Is Right

7

FOCUS

"People think focus means saying yes to the thing you've got to focus on. But that's not what it means at all. It means saying no to the hundred other good ideas that there are. You have to pick carefully."
— Steve Jobs

When we started Bright Bear, we were willing to work for basically anyone with a checkbook. We even took on a few residential customers, which were always a lot of effort for a very small, usually singular payout. Later on, we chose to refer all residential business to a trusted provider known for quality work. We also did websites. And some graphic design. In our first year in business, I took home about $17,000 in pay. Not exactly living the dream, but I was certainly working hard at it.

I remember in one of the networking groups that I was working with, there was a handyman who told us that we should think of him as our own personal MacGyver. MacGyver, in case you're not as old as I am, was a television show where a mulleted Richard Dean Anderson would get into a pickle, and then get himself out of it with science know-how, mechanical intelligence, and explosions.

MacGyver hated guns, preferring science demonstrations that took at least two commercial breaks to explain and execute.

After explaining his evil plan, the criminal would say something like, "Okay, MacGyver. I've finally captured you, but I'm not going to kill you yet. Instead, I'm going to lock you in a room full of scientific contraptions and toxic chemicals and just see what happens."

But the point is that television's MacGyver, among his many skills, could fix anything. In one egg-citing hard boiled episode, he starts up a car that hasn't run in decades by cracking eggs and putting them in the radiator, where the heat causes the eggs to cook and seal a leak long enough for the car to be driven to safety.

So, when this guy compared himself to television's MacGyver, my expectations were stratospheric. When it came to the part of the meeting where you get to talk about your business, it became clear that he wasn't just a handyman; he was a one-man Swiss Army knife. He would start listing all of the things he could do, which was everything under the sun. He could hang a television, he could rebuild a transmission, he could cater your next family party. He was probably really smart and highly skilled, but I noticed he wasn't getting a lot of referrals from the group. He wanted us to mentally file his business under "miscellaneous." That approach, however, didn't seem particularly effective.

There was also a home and auto insurance company that offered all kinds of other services, including banking, investment products, and life insurance. They were sternly advised to pick one category, and the reason for this wasn't to limit their success, but to improve their odds of wanting to renew their membership.

The shotgun approach isn't memorable. The worst thing you could say in one of those groups was "we're looking for a referral to businesses in the area" because that would make people think of exactly zero potential referrals. You'd do better choosing a vertical at random. "We're focusing this week on dental practices and orthodontists," someone might say. Now everyone has a name in mind. I used to tell people to remember that "specific is terrific."

While there might be a lot of things that you can do, it's important to become the one that people think of when a topic comes up. It's so important to have a focus. You ask me for someone who can fix a Jaguar, or a trust attorney, or a low voltage cabling contractor, and I know exactly whom you should call. Ask me for a business in the area, and even if I manage to think of one, it's probably not the one you really want. It's like when you're going out to lunch with someone, and you ask what they're in the mood for, and they say "anything." It's annoying.

It's also important to be specific about who your customers are.

The first time I stumbled into what is called a "vertical," a specific category of customers, was when the finance director of the local chapter of a nationally known nonprofit was looking for some help with IT. He vetted us thoroughly. Not only asked us for references, but showed up at their offices and asked to see the IT closet. He came to our office as well, which at the time was shared with my partner's father's landscaping company. It was a reasonably nice office that smelled faintly of manure and gasoline.

Finally, he decided he was satisfied, and consequently he agreed to set up a meeting for us with the CEO. I recall the CEO had been some sort of professional athlete. I remember his enormous hand wrapping around mine for a handshake when we walked into his office. I might have been more nervous if I didn't have a couple aces up my sleeve.

After the initial pleasantries, he started explaining the challenges they were having. They had an on-premise email server that needed to be replaced, and their IT provider was quoting $35,000 for the parts and labor. They were also looking for a way to reduce what they were paying so that they could get more funding into programs that would benefit the community.

"Have you heard of the California Teleconnect Fund," I asked him?

He had not. So I turned to the director of finance and asked him if it would be possible to take a look at their last phone and internet bill. He returned in less than two minutes with a folded piece of paper.

"Take a look at the bottom of the bill, where they hit you with all those little fees and charges. Do you see something that says CTF?"

"Here it is. $9. But what I really care about is this bill is almost two thousand dollars. I don't think nine dollars is going to make much difference."

"Sir, that $9 you paid goes into a state fund that is redistributed to nonprofits. Participating nonprofits can use those funds to pay up to 50% of their bill. I think you belong on the receiving end of that."

"I think I like this guy already," he said.

"And I understand you're in the market for a new email server," I asked?

"Here it comes," he replied. "I know that's not going to be cheap."

"I expect we can get you qualified for Google Apps for Nonprofits, which would allow you to keep your domain and use Google's system for email, at no cost. You'd want to migrate your email data from your on premise server to Google, which is something we can help you with."

That became a significant account for us, and it led to several others. Their logo at the time was designed by Norman Rockwell. Their organization was featured in an episode of The West Wing. They had a sterling reputation in the community and nationwide. And it was looked up to by all the other local nonprofit organizations. When people asked "who else do you work with?" We had a really good answer to that question. Moreover, nonprofit boards are generally populated by their most generous donors, who tend to be people who are also operating successful businesses that need IT services.

This became a viable playbook. We would get meetings with nonprofit organizations, enroll them in the teleconnect fund and Google for Nonprofits, become their trusted IT provider, and ask them for referrals. After a few years, we had talked to almost every nonprofit organization in the area, and many of them decided to work with us.

Most salespeople hear the word "nonprofit" and they think someone has just said "no money," and while it's true that nonprofit organizations are value oriented, you can pull their 990 forms, which are usually right there on their public website, and see how much revenue they have, which is frequently a multiple of millions of dollars. Just like any other organization, they have operating costs, and who needs IT security more than an organization that is storing the personally identifying information of vulnerable children?

The trick to working with a nonprofit is that you have to make the sale twice. First you need to sell the staff, then you have to help them sell you to their board. It's helpful if you can find some cost savings out of the gate, and the teleconnect fund and Google Apps for Nonprofits were usually enough to get me a second meeting. The sales cycle is long. A regular business would sometimes hire us on the spot. Nonprofit organizations always took longer to decide, sometimes up to six months. By then a lot of our competitors would have written them off.

Doing this work also helped with morale. In between the lawyers and accountants, our techs might pick up a service call for a field worker at a high school who was trying to enroll kids in a hiking trip and needed some help with a spreadsheet question. Helping someone who was directly involved in positively impacting the world would put a lift in their step for the rest of the day. We started living vicariously through their successes.

This account changed the way we did business. Not only did we have a strategy that made sense with a lot of blue sky in front of us, but people started talking about us in the nonprofit community. We became known as "That IT company that works with nonprofits" and every account we got into gave us more specialized knowledge that made us even more valuable. Nonprofits have their own language, their own odd software like "The Raiser's Edge," and their own set of unique challenges. I got to a point where I understood enough that I had useful advice to give a grant writer, and they just weren't going to get that from any other IT service provider in town.

We also enjoyed participating in their events. We would show up at their fundraisers, volunteer for their programs, and enjoy being part of their team. One year, a customer had a Halloween costume contest at their office, and some of the contestants dressed up as us. They were wearing our black polo shirts and carrying keyboards. One of our technicians had a distinctive tattoo shaped like the state of California on his forearm, and someone at the nonprofit had drawn that on with a sharpie. I think they won third place.

I loved all of the nonprofits, and we were even starting to get inquiries from nonprofits in other states, but one of my favorites was just around the corner. Free Wheelchair Mission was founded by Don Schoendorfer, an engineer who saw a big problem in the world that he wanted to fix: there are people in developing countries who can't walk, and don't have access to a wheelchair, so they just exist on the ground, crawling to their destination, relying on family to carry them, or just staying still.

Don wanted to use technology to move people. And you already know how I feel about that. His first prototype looked like a plastic lawn chair strapped to a dismembered bicycle, but Don understood cost per unit and value engineering, and each new generation of wheelchair looked more comfortable and more rugged. His pitch was that you could change someone's life for less than $100. How many times would you like to do that today?

Don also believed in what engineers call "dogfooding," which means he tested his own product. If the chair was good enough for the people he served, it was good enough for him. So he used one of his wheelchairs as a desk chair. One of our technicians just about fainted from shock when he saw Don casually stand up and walk away from his wheelchair.

After I sold my business, I celebrated by buying a bunch of wheelchairs for people I will never meet on this side of heaven. My dad also challenged me to split the cost of digging a well and providing clean water for a community in Uganda, so we did that too. It was during Covid, so we didn't get to go to the celebration when it was dedicated, but I'd like to go see it someday.

One time, we got a call from an escrow company. In New York, they use attorneys to accomplish this instead, but in many U.S. States, including California, when you buy a house, the buyer deposits funds in a special account before they are dispersed to the seller. Usually there is a deposit, or earnest money, some costs that have to be paid like the brokers' commissions and inspection fees, any mortgages are paid off, and eventually the remaining balance needs to get to the person who is selling the house. Escrow officers manage billions of dollars, and have to know a lot about banking and real estate to serve their customers well.

The first escrow company we worked with found us on Google. For all the effort I put into organic search engine optimization, it's one of the only times a customer found us that way. They immediately asked us for a meeting.

The CEO was sick, but he dragged himself to the office to meet us, and I managed to get a fist bump from him. We talked about our service offerings, and they were interested, and before I knew it we had a new customer, one of the largest independent escrow companies in Southern California.

A few months later, we started working with them on SOC1 and SOC2 compliance, which is an AICPA program designed for banking and financial institutions and their service providers. Learning how to do that proved to be important later.

The CFO of that company somehow ended up working for a different escrow company, and it turned out that they also needed help with IT. And it turns out that escrow officers change affiliations as often as realtors, so soon we had several escrow companies working with us, and I found myself speaking at conferences to escrow officers about IT security.

This was really, really effective. Escrow companies were

seeking us out, and every customer we signed up made us even more valuable to them, because these were challenging accounts that required specialized knowledge with real security, compliance, and business problems to solve.

Once, on a brisk fall morning before I had finished my second cup of coffee, I answered my phone and found myself talking to the CEO and COO of an escrow company, as well as the Chief Information Security Officer and IT Director of a regional bank that you've definitely heard of, and they were all yelling at me. Someone had sent an email to the bank with phony wire transfer instructions from what appeared to be an escrow officer's company email account, but the escrow officer had no knowledge of it. They weren't asking me for advice. They were demanding that I shut down the entire system so that no email could be sent out, requiring a full security audit, and advising me that we might become the subject of litigation.

I asked them to send me the email. As soon as I saw the email, I started laughing. They did not appreciate my response. I said, "Hey guys, how do you spell escrow?"

The attacker had purchased a new domain name, replacing "escrow" in their name with "escroow" the day before, and signed up for a new Office 365 account, and then began committing criminal acts of fraud. My college job as a proofreader might have saved me at that moment. The attackers got details of the transaction from the realtor, (It was always the realtor. jennsellshomez123@aol.com never seemed to have MFA enabled.) spent $25 on Godaddy services, and went in for the kill. There was no hacking involved, just some creative spelling and social engineering.

At that point, I took control of the conversation. I told the bank's IT personnel that I was going to restrict all email traffic from my customer to their bank, that all mail would arrive encrypted from now on, and that they would have to go to a special portal to read the messages. "This way if you get any email that appears to be from my customer in plain text with no encrypted portal required, you'll know it's an attack."

This was not the first or last time IT security professionals listened to my advice. I was becoming perceived as an expert, because I had learned to be specific.

More succinctly, as one of my eloquent professors was fond of saying, "niches make riches, bitches."

After 10 years, we had a lot of customers, but most of them were small accounts. A handful of them were very good accounts that all of our competitors would have loved to pitch to. I had tried to treat them all the same, giving even the smallest accounts the benefit of our hard-won compliance and security protocols. Small companies who got our firewall probably had no idea that it had passed an annual penetration test, where a certified ethical hacker had put it through its paces, and that it was defending billions of dollars of transactions on public and private networks, capable of multiple layers of strong encryption on thousands of simultaneous communications.

I never fired customers. My mentality in the early years was that we were so lean that we simply could not lose an account, so I would do whatever I had to do to retain them. Later on, I felt like it was ethical to "dance with the girl you brought to the dance," and remained fiercely loyal to people who believed in us before it really made sense to. I saw this as virtuous. My staff saw it as crazy.

They were probably right.

For one thing, there are providers who focus on entry level accounts, and those accounts might prefer a provider that depends on their business as much as they depend on their provider. I was taking opportunities away from startup providers in my market who not only might have done a good job, but who needed the work. Instead, I was burning the candle at both ends and stubbornly not letting go of anything, at great personal and professional cost. Even after the sale of our business, I stayed on with the new owners and took care of some of those accounts for a couple of years.

One day, I remember I was sitting in the conference room at the new owner's beautiful new headquarters, and we were going over some numbers in a sales meeting. I had a dashboard built that showed me the revenue performance of all of the companies that had been my customers before the acquisition, and I realized that the 80/20 rule, the principle that 80% of your revenue comes from 20% of your customers, was literally true. I could have referred away 80% of the calls, the noise, the interruptions and power outages, and focused on just 20% of our customers, and had such an easy go of it.

I'm not saying you should hastily fire a bunch of customers this afternoon, but maybe it's not an act of kindness to make your smallest customers wait for your limited attention. Maybe it's not kind to you or to them. Some of those accounts were not very profitable, some of them didn't realize how valuable we were, and all of them were a lot of work. I was proud of the fact that I had failed to focus, and was giving relatively equal amounts of attention and service quality to small accounts and large ones.

I was so myopic that I hadn't realized it might have been a viable option to reduce the number of accounts we were servicing, let some agreements expire instead of renew, and reduce the amount of stress and anxiety we were carrying. A better leader might have figured that out faster. It was a hard lesson for me to learn.

Focus

8

THE SORCERER'S APPRENTICE

"To laugh at yourself is to love yourself."
— Mickey Mouse

In Walt Disney's Fantasia, a stern-faced sorcerer is heading out of his lair, and asks his apprentice, Mickey Mouse, to tidy up while he's away. Mickey puts on the sorcerer's massive hat, considers a room full of chores, and has an idea. Eyes wide with excitement, he flicks his fingers, bringing a broom to life. Its wooden limbs march stiffly, dutifully hauling water to mop the floors. For a moment, everything moves in perfect, mechanical harmony. The broom multiplies, and what began as a whimsical dance quickly descends into disaster, the once-quiet space now roaring with relentless, unstoppable, automated chaos. Drenched and desperate, Mickey watches his plan unravel, as he is swallowed by a flood of his own creation.

Although Fantasia was released in 1940, each cell painstakingly illustrated and painted to create the illusion of movement, it touches on fears that people have about automation today, especially as humanity learns to contend with large language models, which marketers have dubbed "Generative AI."

A couple years after I sold my business, I accepted a job with a company that was focused on helping small businesses apply for a generous federal tax credit that had been designed to help them contend with the economic impact of the Covid 19 pandemic.

We had a team of developers working on automating several aspects of the process, in an effort to improve the number of businesses we were able to serve before the program deadline.

At one point, I encountered a sentiment-driven argument that we should not rely on automation because it would reduce the number of jobs that we could create.

So I said, "OK, let's play that logic backwards." I suggested that we would need more people to do the same amount of work if, instead of using computers to prepare tax paperwork, we insisted that all of the tax worksheets would be completed by hand with number 2 pencils, the way people used to do it.

"But there's a catch," I said.

"Since we won't be able to process as many returns without software, we won't have as much revenue, and so I'm afraid we will have to let some people go. See, when you take away technology, the value of an employee is reduced, because they can't create as much production without that leverage."

"Conversely," I argued, "if one person can create more production, is that person worth more to the company as a result of automation or less?" More, of course. In every case, throughout history, there are better jobs on the other side of automation, however people are still terrified of it.

The first steamship was smashed to pieces in the middle of the night by oarsmen with their oars, fearing obsolescence. The first loom was destroyed by weavers. If you've seen the film *Hidden Figures* about the early years of the space program, you'll see that NASA had employees who did hard math problems and those people were called "computers."

But what about generative "AI?" Isn't it going to take away all our jobs?

Guy Kawasaki has one of my favorite takes on this: He talks about ice technology. See, a long time ago, people would drive their horse and buggy into the middle of a frozen lake, saw out a chunk of frozen water, and drive it into the town square. For a penny, they would cut you a piece of it, and you could watch it melt in your hands, or perhaps put it in a box with some fresh meat and keep it fresh for an extra day. The beginning of ice technology.

Then they figured out how to build a factory that could remove heat from water, and in the space of a single city block, they could transform ordinary water into ice. A quantum leap in ice technology. Ice men, wearing pressed uniforms bleached white, would bring a block of ice and carefully use sterilized ice tongs to place it in your insulated ice box.

More recently, as you are aware, the ice factory has been miniaturized, and I now have a tiny ice factory inside my "ice box." Refrigerators are a curve jumping, paradigm shattering, incredible advance in ice technology. The fact that you can get ice cubes on demand in your kitchen should fill you with a sense of wonder and amazement.

You could look at this series of events and protest that

the buggy driver lost his job, and the ice men are probably not in high demand anymore, however people are still engineering, building, selling, and installing refrigerators. More importantly, refrigeration improves food safety and makes it possible to eat fresh blueberries in Phoenix and Sushi in Des Moines. The technology caught on because it improves our outcomes.

If you buy a new refrigerator and you want your ice maker to work in an old house, you're going to have to hire someone to retrofit a water line. A lot of people went out and bought new refrigerators. Moreover, while ice delivery perhaps isn't the growth industry it once was, logistics is still a pretty good way to earn a living. Maybe the ice men's offspring sold appliances at Sears, or maybe they delivered other products or services.

The oarsmen and weavers had nothing to fear. The weavers' knowledge and skill became more valuable with each generation of automation that came along. Because they knew how the thread and yarn needed to come together to make fabric. They could see what needed to happen to make quality apparel, and when we armed them with automation, they had the creative vision to do more daring things with cotton and polyester than anyone ever thought possible

Some of the oarsmen might have clung to their oars, and reacted by discounting the price of a human-powered ferry ride across the Mississippi to compete with the steamships, but some of them must have successfully captained larger vessels than they could have previously been able to fathom, with the hard won knowledge of currents and propulsion gained by decades of doing it the hard way.

There are always better jobs on the other side of automation.

But let's talk specifically about "AI."

I put that in quotes because it's a lie, and I want to tell you the truth. It's not intelligent. Large language models (LLMs) can't plan or dream or want things. They lack judgment. The language models translate words into tokens and manipulate those tokens with algebra to guess, one word at a time, what the next word in the sentence should be.

The grandfather of these language models was the predictive text engine on your T9 Nokia phone in 2003. If you're not old enough to remember this time, as we tapped the same button three times to key in a single letter, the phone would mercifully guess what your next word might be. "I'm going to the-" you'd type, excruciatingly slowly, and the phone would suggest the word "store" which you could accept or overwrite with lots of button presses. Even if you weren't planning on going to the store, it might be easier to stop there than to type out the word you originally intended.

How did it know? Was it magic? Not really. It turned language into a math problem, and computers are good at math.

It knew that "store" was what you were going to say because that is the word that most likely comes next in the context you provided.

Similarly, TikTok knows you like anthropomorphic kittens and burnout videos because when it serves up one of those videos, you stare at them a little longer than the other ones.

There is one kind of answer that LLM's are very good at providing:

A consensus answer.

An LLM can respond to stimulus and provide a consensus answer. LLMs would win every game of Family Feud, and always pick the best answers in order. Getting it to do something that even resembles novelty requires some creative prompt writing, and the results will often be unsatisfactory.

The same thing that makes humans bad at Family Feud is what makes us good at creating things. The survey says that the best answer to "something you find in a drug store" is drugs. A human might say "a humidifier." And suddenly we are engaged in a completely different way, because humanity isn't uniform. We all have different perspectives and experiences that we bring to what we create. We can surprise you and say something unexpected.

"AI" is essentially a calculator for words, and while that is consequential, game-changing, curve-jumping, world altering technology, it isn't a replacement for human creativity. But maybe it can become an amplifier.

Another reason LLMs are contentious is because they

sometimes hallucinate. They might tell you things that are demonstrably false. For example, the quote at the beginning of chapter 3? It's not real. I used an LLM to find it, and when I asked it to provide a citation, it reluctantly admitted that it made the whole thing up.

This exchange may give you some insight into how it works. Here's how it explained why it lied to me:

"It looks like the quote might have been generated or adapted in our conversation as a creative interpretation rather than being sourced from an existing text. The quote reflects the dual nature of California as both a land of opportunity and a place where the pursuit of dreams can come with significant challenges, which aligns with themes often explored in stories about life in California.

The structure of the quote-with the idea of dreams requiring "an extra large maintenance contract"—is a metaphorical way to express that achieving and maintaining success in California often demands considerable effort and resources. This kind of language is typical of how we might describe the contrasts in places like California, where the dream is alluring but not without its costs. It seems to have been created in the context of discussing Beverly Hills, 90210 and California's image, possibly as an imagined line that could fit within those themes. I'm glad you found it intriguing!

The quote emerged as a creative synthesis rather than being sourced from a specific episode or literary work. Here's a breakdown of how the elements of the quote come together:

1. *"Welcome to California: a land of dreams":*

- *California has long been romanticized as a place where dreams can come true, from the Gold Rush era to Hollywood's glitz and the tech boom in Silicon Valley. This phrase taps into that historical and cultural narrative, positioning California as a destination synonymous with ambition and opportunity.*

2. *"but dreams are dangerous commodities":*

- *This part of the quote introduces a cautionary note. While dreams are valuable and desirable, they can also be fraught with risk. This reflects the idea that pursuing big dreams, particularly in a competitive and high-stakes environment like California, can be perilous. It echoes a common theme in literature and media, where the pursuit of success often comes with unforeseen challenges.*

3. *"they usually require an extra large maintenance contract":*

- *The metaphor of a "maintenance contract" adds a practical, almost business-like perspective to the dream. It suggests that achieving and maintaining one's dreams requires ongoing effort, resources, and perhaps sacrifices. This imagery is reminiscent of the reality that in places like California, sustaining success- whether in Hollywood, Silicon Valley, or any other industry- often involves significant investment and vigilance.*

The quote was crafted in response to a request for quotes

from the pilot of Beverly Hills, 90210. While discussing the themes of California as depicted in the show, this phrase encapsulates the dichotomy of California's allure and the challenges it presents.

It was constructed to evoke the style and thematic elements often found in dialogues about California, particularly in media that explores its culture, such as Beverly Hills, 90210. The language mirrors the show's blend of aspiration and realism, making it feel like something a character might say when reflecting on the experience of moving to or living in California."

Then I scolded it.

"It's great that you're able to do that, but you need to let people know when you're doing it. When people ask for a quote from a specific episode of a specific show, you might say 'I can't find a great example in the script, but I can imagine one that might sound like this:'

I know it's sometimes hard to tell, but sometimes humans will want you to be creative, and sometimes they will want you to be accurate. If you're not sure, it's better to ask."

The screen flashed with a message that said "memory updated" and it promised me that it would try to do better in the future.

What's really interesting to me about that exchange is that subsequently when I asked it for quotes that it couldn't find, instead of making one up, on a couple of occasions it would ask me if I preferred a real quote that didn't quite match my criteria or an imaginary one like the one Brandon Walsh never said.

That's a problem, though. LLMs generate responses based on patterns instead of understanding. Relying on LLMs, attorneys in court have cited legal precedents that don't exist. Preachers have quoted from the book of Hezekiah (there isn't one) and I'm sure lots of people have relied on terrible consensus advice, because the weighted average of all the ideas on the internet isn't always a high quality idea. In several cases, people successfully trained an LLM with white supremacist ideology. Google developers reacted to this, and forced their fledgling LLM not to be racist, so then Bard started suggesting that many of America's founding fathers and even Presidents were Native American, in a botched effort at inclusivity.

LLMs are, like most technology, force multipliers. They're not great at being spontaneously creative, but when they intuit that we want them to be, they have to be able to consider things that don't already exist. These models hallucinate because we sometimes make demands of them that require them to have a tenuous grip on reality, and they lack the judgment to know the difference between a situation when we want them to be "creative" and a situation when we are relying on the model for accuracy.

I think a very important question to ask about new technology is: "What is this technology for?"

The microwave oven was invented by Percy Spencer when he was experimenting with radio towers at Raytheon. He was fond of an afternoon snack, and the chocolate bar in his pocket kept melting when he was working near active microwave radio communication equipment. He sold the rights and design for the first microwave oven to General Electric for $50,000. Dr. Spencer Silver was a chemist at 3M who was trying to create a strong adhesive. His work was considered a failure until someone realized that being able to stick something on to a piece of paper temporarily and remove it easily was a feature, not a bug. His Post-It Notes are one of 3M's most recognizable products today.

WD-40, the household lubricant that's as ubiquitous as duct tape, is named for the fortieth attempt at a chemical formula for water displacement. Viagra was intended to treat cardiac blood vessels until they realized it had another, um, straightforward use.

Blockchain technology has been around for several years now, and everyone seems to think it's for money. There are several tokenized public ledgers where people can move virtual tokens transactionally, and people built massive server farms to find each new crypto currency's "coins" before they are all discovered.

But I don't think semi-anonymous money is what blockchain is really for. I say blockchain is for knowing things that are true. Because blockchain is a public ledger, it can be used, for example, to prove that something was in a particular place at a particular time. Blockchain can tell you with certainty about the supply chain for what you're feeding your children. It can establish a chain of custody. You can know that your coffee really was harvested in Columbia and roasted at a certified fair trade facility in Honduras before it arrived in the port of Los Angeles exactly 7 weeks before it arrived at the local farmer's market. Blockchain could tell you definitively if your kid's apple juice is from Vermont or Guangdong. Blockchain could end the scourge of child slavery by compelling suppliers to be transparent about where our stuff comes from and who made it. Money is neither a creative use of blockchain, nor a particularly durable one.

I don't know what LLMs are for yet, but I have some ideas. They're good at automating repetitive tasks and pattern recognition. What if an LLM could analyze the DNA of a particular person's carcinoma cell and develop a personalized MRNA vaccine? Perhaps an LLM could accomplish in moments a task that would take a team of scientists dozens of years: designing a vaccine to fight one person's unique and proprietary cancer. This is the sort of possibility that I think might be on the horizon.

LLMs are not good at poetry, but they are good at averaging together information to generate a consensus answer. We mustn't rely on them to think for us. No. But they can create a baseline that we can move beyond.

What I mean is, students shouldn't delegate their essays to an LLM, because as several grumpy educators have explained to me, there is necessary and constructive friction for students that happens when they are thinking through their assignments. But the really smart ones might have the LLM generate a consensus paper and then, armed with the knowledge of what their comparatively average classmates are going to turn in, challenge themselves to write something much better, because frequently the Family Feud answer, or the design by committee visual that you're going to get by averaging other people ideas, is at best mediocre, and at worst, wrong. It's a starting point, not the destination. Blockchain is for knowing things that are true. One use of LLMs might be averaging available information to identify consensus.

As one person on Facebook put it, "I want AI to do my laundry so I can make art, not make art so I can do laundry." Technology is a force multiplier. It will do what we ask of it. So let's tell it to do some laundry.

We had some fun with automation in our business. We had a "technician" named Alfred P Inglesby, a silly name with the initials API, which really stands for "application programming interface." APIs are used by programmers to connect different kinds of software together. For example, we had monitoring on our endpoints that would alert us to common problems, like a hard drive that was running out of space. Old Alfred would get the alert that someone's disk was nearly full, and he would tell our agent to run a script that would empty the trash and clear out temp files and delete old logs, in an effort to keep the system running without human intervention, before the customer even realized there was a problem. It was as simple as "if this happens, do this." One of two things would happen. If the script fixed the issue, "Alfred" would note the ticket and mark it complete. If it didn't, he'd assign it to a technician to follow up. Alfred was frequently our top performing technician, but he was really just a bunch of conditional "if" statements. If drive full, then run script. If drive not full anymore, then paste text and close ticket. If script not work, tell service desk. My poodle is exponentially smarter than that script, but sometimes when I explain things like that to people, they look at me as if I've spontaneously created a life form *ex nihilo*.

Conditional statements are not alive. Logic is not the same thing as intelligence. Those statements should be uncontroversial.

A few years ago, there were a lot of smart software developers in Ukraine advertising their services on Upwork and other gig websites. I hired one of them to solve a problem we were having with a Citrix server. I don't know if he's still alive, but if he is, I imagine he's using what he knows about technology as a force multiplier in warfare. Ukrainian developers have programmed inexpensive and readily available toy drones to swarm prey, carry payloads, recognize hidden caches, and follow and attack moving targets, summarily using pattern recognition to automate death. They will not be the last people to do this. We need to develop standards for the ethical use of AI, because automating death seems like it might turn out worse than Mickey Mouse's attempts at automating janitorial work. If you give LLMs a license to kill based on pattern recognition, that's essentially automating profiling with fatal consequences.

When you're automating something, it's important to really solidify and lock down your manual process first, and try it a bunch of times until you can anticipate all the exceptions that might come up, and then figure out how to handle those. Like Mickey, we can get in serious trouble if we skip that step. Really nailing down the manual process, carefully isolating and automating stages of that process, and lots of testing and exception handling are necessary steps before you type "run" and press enter on any kind of automation. We must learn from Disney's cautionary tale, and consider what's going to happen before we decide to casually multiply the effect of our actions by 10x. Humanity is growing into this, and I expect some contemporary equivalents of oarsmen and weavers will try to slow us down before we figure this out. Maybe this time we need them to.

The Sorcerer's Apprentice

9

FAILURE IS OPTIONAL

It's just an old beat up truck
Some say that I should trade up
Now that I got some jangle in my pocket
But what they don't understand
Is it's the miles that make a man
I wouldn't trade that thing in for a rocket
What they don't know is my dad and me
We drove her out to Tennessee
She's still here, and now he's gone
So I hold on
   — Dierks Bentley

After the sale of Bright Bear, I relocated my family to West Linn, Oregon, a small Portland suburb quite near the end of the Oregon Trail. In fact, be careful what video games you let your kids play, because at some point it occurred to me that the view that was animated into the pixilated victory screen you saw at the end of the computer game if you managed to avoid dysentery and starvation was just a short walk from our house. We bought a place with more land than I thought I'd ever own, a creek running through the back yard, 70 foot tall redwood trees, and a four car tandem garage for our new boat with a free public boat launch into the Willamette River just a few minutes from our driveway.

We built a fire pit next to the creek and ordered ourselves a fancy hot tub. It was wonderful there when it wasn't over a hundred degrees.

See, the house was built in the 1950s, and one small problem: it didn't have air conditioning. I bought three portable air conditioners from the local hardware store, but the house was about 4600 square feet, so we could only cool a couple of rooms, and only by about 20 degrees. If it was 90 out, we were in good shape. If it was 105, it was still rather uncomfortable indoors. One Friday afternoon, I realized that the forecast for Saturday was 116 degrees. I pictured the four of us sitting directly in front of the little air conditioner, breathing 96 degree air indoors.

I suggested to Kelly that we should buy airline tickets, right now, and just go somewhere cooler for a few days. We picked San Diego, where it was overcast and 65 degrees. Back home in Oregon, there were power outages, convenience stores ran out of ice, and a few people died in the extreme heat. The city opened "cooling centers" and people crowded into high school gymnasiums and public libraries and waited for the heat to break. I feel confident that we made the right choice in giving up and leaving town.

We looked down the barrel of a sticky, sweaty weekend and realized it was optional.

After the acquisition closed, the new owners of Bright Bear seemed to be pleased with their purchase, but some of their existing staff didn't welcome me with open arms. Over time, I gradually won most of them over, but I remember a conversation with another manager there who said I sometimes reminded him of a pitbull.

"Thanks," I said sincerely.

"It wasn't exactly a compliment," he replied.

"Well, thank you for your candor then."

One of my responsibilities was datacenter consolidation. My company had assets in two datacenters in two different states, and the acquiring company had infrastructure in a third location. We also had a recovery cloud for failover purposes set up in a fourth datacenter. There was an argument for keeping two sites, but a third was unnecessary, and four was bordering on inefficient. The date for moving kept getting pushed back again and again, until I grew frustrated, pulled rank, and told them I was coming down there with a power drill to start taking things apart and moving them myself. Ultimately someone relented, I got what I wanted, and the infrastructure traveled to its new home with no customer impact and minimal friction. The owners were happy with the result.

I remember so many times in my career when I eventually succeeded even though giving up would have been an understandable and normal response. Like that other manager said, I would bite down and not let go, like a pitbull, until I achieved the result I needed to achieve. That tenacity was annoying to the people I worked with, but it's one of the reasons we made it. I realized that often in technology there is more than one right answer, so if you just keep pressing in, eventually you'll find a configuration or a combination of variables that's serviceable. I remember spending a weekend in San Francisco at a customer's office trying to bring up a dead phone system and succeeding at 3am on Monday morning. A week of late nights in Minnesota troubleshooting DNS resolution issues and installing wireless access points on a 30 foot high ceiling, a projector install where we failed to plan for electricity beforehand. An email server that wouldn't boot. Over and over, I shouldn't have succeeded, but I bit down and held on.

Once, we had to install internet and phones at a job site in downtown Los Angeles, and the city refused to let our internet vendor dig up Grand Avenue to run new fiber for our customer. We showed up with a pair of wireless microwave transceivers and beamed the internet from an apartment building across the street over the traffic below, and used a picture of me aiming the dish in our marketing materials.

Later, at the same project, I took on an unusual project and built a 144 square foot display out of nine giant televisions from Costco, one trash can shaped Mac Pro, three Matrox TripleHead2Go adapters, and the excellent ProVideoPlayer by Renewed Vision Software. It was as big as a billboard. You could see it quite clearly from across the street. I turned up the brightness and contrast until it scorched the eyeballs of everyone passing by. They told me later that my bid was one third of what they expected to pay.

For better or worse, once I decide to do something, it's very hard for me to accept anything other than unqualified success.

In the early years of my business, when several of my friends encouraged me to quit, I paid the bills with side hustles. I worked two days a week at a church, sold cars, and taught business networking classes. It was hard. I remember cashing a $75 check I earned for a couple days of work and immediately using the money to buy groceries. I would pick up the ad by the front door and only buy things that were loss leaders. One time my wife wanted hummus, and I made it myself out of canned chickpeas to save two dollars. I changed my own oil and spark plugs. We didn't have cable TV. Still don't, technically, although now there are so many streaming services that we might as well have cable.

Dierks Bentley sings a song about holding on. I'm slow to appreciate most country music, but I love that song. Summarily, he tells his partner that since he won't give up on his classic truck or his old guitar, he's certainly not going to give up on her.

My wife and I celebrated our twenty-first wedding anniversary the other day, and I'd be lying if I said it was always easy, because I assure you that being married to me isn't, but the best things in life are usually not easy. The things we've been through together have allowed us to make a life that is as imperfect as it is beautiful. I've heard that sometimes people now say in their wedding vows something to the effect of "as long as our love doth last" and that's just not how I manage the important things in my life. I don't give up on people or ideas easily, for better or worse. For richer or poorer, for that matter. Frequently poorer.

Don't misunderstand, divorce is far better than murder, and I've seen more than a few situations up close where divorce was the best available option for everyone involved, but I can say that I've never seriously considered or suggested it for Kelly and I, even in the wake of our worst arguments. I've said and done things I'm ashamed of, and I'm far from being a perfect husband, but I have no interest in or even comprehension of a future where I am still drawing breath but not married to my best friend. I told Kelly on our wedding day that "I would rather struggle with you than prosper without you." I have tested the limits of that sentiment on several occasions. My friend Phil Putnam once told me that love "is like settling into something that's always been true." I think about that idea all the time. I've never been a person who struggles with commitment.

I was a pitbull in business because I love my family. I'd like to think I became that for them. Because they needed me to succeed, I refused to fail. When we found out that our second son was on the way, we were emotionally ready, but not financially ready to have a second baby. Even though I hadn't met him yet, there was no way I was going to let that kid down.

Sometimes that intensity made me a hard person to be around. Frequently, I can be kind of a lot. But like that guy with the dirty truck and the old guitar, I insistently bite down and hold on. That might also be a character flaw, but in hindsight it's undeniably one of the reasons why the plan worked, and probably why I instinctively didn't want to commit to more than ten years of running that business in the first place. I knew I would somehow manage to do what I set out to do, no matter what it cost, even against unreasonable odds. If you're like me in this way, your odds of success in a startup are probably at least double.

10

YOU CAN BUY CUSTOMERS

"People don't care about your business. They care about their problems. Be the solution that they're looking for."
— Melonie Dodaro

After our company was acquired, I worked for the buyers for a couple of years. Subsequently I became CIO of a company that grew from 50 people to over a thousand in just a few months by helping small businesses claim pandemic related tax credits. To accomplish this, we did a lot of advertising. Our monthly ad spend at one point was roughly equal to Domino's Pizza's annual advertising spend, and the reason behind that was that our CAC, the cost of acquiring a customer, was small in comparison to the value of the relationships we were creating.

While our CAC might have been astronomical for most businesses, the math worked fine for us. My boss had previously worked for PWC, Fiserv, JP Morgan Chase, and NASA. Our CMO was previously VP of Marketing for Petsmart. We hired a spokesperson that most people in America would immediately recognize, and made memorable commercials that aired during prime time and sporting events. We were profiled in the Wall Street Journal. I felt as if I had joined the Beatles and I was Ringo Starr, just trying to keep time with a stupid grin on my face, happy to be among some of what I considered to be some of the greatest minds of my generation.

Sitting around a giant conference table in the ninth tallest building in Florida, I received a crash course in marketing.

The concept of a sales funnel wasn't new to me. I'd learned about that in several places, particularly during my time in the Goldman Sachs 10,000 Small Businesses program. Marketing qualified leads convert to sales qualified leads, which convert to signed agreements, documents uploaded, work product completed, invoices issued, and receivables collected. At that company the process had about 30 steps. In my subsequent executive role, I simplified it to ten.

You track conversions at each stage of the funnel, monitor for changes, A/B test ideas, and keep refining the process until the machine is working to your satisfaction. Best of all, you can take your profit at the end and feed it back in to create more leads.

What I'd never witnessed before was how well it could work. We would decide how many businesses we wanted to work with in a given month, staff up accordingly, and then buy the correct number of leads to generate that number of conversions. It was so much simpler than I had been led to believe. Once we had a representative sample of data, it was just a math problem.

"You're telling me we can just buy customers," I asked?

They looked at me like I imagine Lennon and McCartney might have often looked at poor old Ringo Starr. "Yeah buddy, that's called marketing."

But yes, it really was that simple, until it wasn't. Eventually, because we kept feeding all of the revenue back into the machine, we started saturating some of the channels that were available to us, so there were constantly new strategies, fresh approaches, and budget re-balancing that was necessary. When my dad mentioned that he heard our commercial six times on his way home from work one day, I realized that we probably had already bought all the customers that terrestrial radio could give us. Channel saturation eventually produces diminishing returns, which is of course a high quality problem - if you can afford to saturate a channel, you're probably doing several things right.

Some of the old channels are slowly dying because new media, digital media, and social media are so addictive and cost effective. Within eight swipes, TikTok has built a profile of you that is astonishingly accurate. They know what you're looking at, and for how long. They algorithmically feed you inconsistent and deliberately addictive dopamine rewards to command your attention so they can sell it to advertisers. Of course there is also credible evidence that the social apps record what you're talking about and process it for keywords even after you put your phone away. You might not care, because they tell you it will only be used to improve your "advertising experience," but the utility of this data is vastly increased when you process it with an LLM, and I consider it likely that it's being used for purposes that might not be in your best interest. If not now, perhaps soon. There's a reason the defense department banned TikTok, and it's not because they hate the Macarena.

If you've never done it before, and you can spare a few minutes, buy an ad.

Whether you're selling products and services or just consuming them, it's a useful exercise to understand how the system works. You can target education levels, age, gender, race, geography, profession, or any combination of the above. And you can get to that level of targeting for a few cents. A fellow named Brian Swichkow started buying ads that were targeting only his roommate, just as a prank. He honed in on the fact that his roommate, a professional sword swallower, had difficulty swallowing pills, an apparent contradiction which he found amusing. He concludes his story, stating "I had effectively driven my roommate to a state of paranoia with Facebook ads, and the entire three week long marketing campaign cost me exactly $1.70."

It's no wonder that radio advertising is getting cheaper. It's nowhere near this efficient.

A caveat: For this idea to be true, that you can buy customers, your product has to generate enough profit to cover the cost of the ad, and your funnel has to be efficient enough that it converts into sales. Put simply, you can't spend $500 on ads to sell one pencil sharpener, but if you could spend $500 on ads that convert into a $10,000 gross sale with 20% net margin, now we're talking.

A CAC of $500 on $2,000 of profit is pretty easy to justify, and while someone with that ratio of ad spend to revenue is probably going to have an easy time of it for a while, it's likely that they will make the mistake of underspending. Once you have identified a favorable ratio like that, you should be solving for other bottlenecks. Can you deliver your product or service to more than a few dozen buyers at a time? If not, what would need to be true for that to happen? More staffing? More automation? Better process? Likely you'll have to go through many iterations to maximize potential, but after many years of doing it the hard way, I was surprised to see how quickly and proficiently professional marketers could fill the top of the funnel with really good leads, using digital marketing.

It was hard to believe in it sometimes. When we were doing hundreds of transactions in a month and talking about thousands, there was some risk involved in staffing and building capacity to meet the demand we were about to create, but over and over again, it worked. I saw it work. The math mathed.

So again, if you suspect that you might be able to pay a few hundred dollars for a new customer, buy an ad. Maybe buy two. Set up a couple campaigns and let your ads compete against each other for your marketing dollars. Spend a few hundred bucks and see if you learn something.

We built our IT business almost entirely on word of mouth and referrals, and while we got a lot of things right, I think we completely missed the opportunity to scale up that business with marketing. Learn from my mistake. Buy digital advertising.

11

THE IRISH GOODBYE

"How lucky I am to have something that makes saying goodbye so hard."
– A.A. Milne, Winnie the Pooh

Let's take a moment to appreciate what might be the most Seinfeld thing Jerry Seinfeld ever did: he walked away. In 1998, Seinfeld was at the top of the heap, dominating TV in a way that's almost unfathomable today. NBC executives are ready to hand him a blank check. "Just keep it going," they say, probably picturing another decade of George's neuroses, Kramer's entrances, and Elaine's terrible dancing. But what does Jerry do? He says, 'Nah, we're done here.' That's not just confidence, that's incredible comedic timing.

For Seinfeld, it wasn't just about the money or the ratings juggernaut that Seinfeld had become. No, it was about knowing when to get out before the magic turned into something less magical. He called it like this: "The biggest thrill wasn't in winning, it was finishing. Seinfeld was a marathon— and you had to know when to get off the course." That's a guy who gets it.

And let's not forget: 76 million people tuned in for that finale. A finale that's still debated and dissected to this day.

Love it or hate it, what matters is that Jerry left on his own terms. No shark-jumping. No forced laughs. Just a clean, deliberate exit. He protected what mattered most: the legacy. It's the ultimate move—make people miss you before they're sick of you.

Jerry's decision to step off the stage when the lights were still bright wasn't just smart—it was iconic. The Seinfeld story has since become a gold standard for leaving with your reputation and your audience's love intact. A masterclass in finishing strong, when almost anyone else would've kept cashing the checks.

Part of the reason we were able to execute our exit was because we started with the end in mind. We picked a timeline. It might have seemed arbitrary to anyone else, but I remember the moment I fixed the idea in my mind.

My Aunt Beth ran a photography studio, Photos By Beth, in downtown Minneapolis. She wasn't my aunt in any biological sense, but since my parents are both only children and so am I, our Thanksgiving turkey was usually more of a Cornish game hen. Beth took an interest in me, and might have been one of the first adults besides my parents to do so. I admired her for starting a business and becoming successful on her own terms.

I was in high school when I asked her how long it took until she knew it was going to work.

"Ten years," she said immediately. "Honestly, most of the first 9 years were pretty rough, but in year 10, we hit our stride, started winning all kinds of awards, and then the referrals poured in. I had to hire twice as many staff just to keep up. There's something about that tenth year."

"And then, did it keep growing exponentially?"

"Not really," she said. "To double in size again, we would have to change a lot of things that I think I've realized kind of make this business special."

Somewhere in the back of my mind, I filed away that idea. Starting a business and running it for 10 years seemed like a good plan. It had worked for Beth. Maybe I could do it too.

The same day Chris and I agreed to seriously pursue the sale of our company, I coincidentally received a call from an investor who was interested in purchasing the business. We didn't know it yet, but 10 years turned out to be fairly good market timing. There was an acquisition spree in our industry. A lot of people were getting out and companies were consolidating. I received over thirty similar calls before we received an LOI that we found acceptable.

Here's a crash course in business valuation. If you can wrap your mind around this, I promise it's worth the entire price of this book. I might be guilty of oversimplifying this a little, but this framework will help you make sense of why this happens in business so often.

To estimate your value, first, you look at your earnings and profit. What the accountants call EBITDA. It turns out that you can manipulate your profitability with financial levers like interest, taxes, depreciation, and amortization, so we toss all of that aside to get to a level playing field. You also might get some "add backs" - If the company leased you a Cybertruck as an executive perk, that's not a normal business expense, and you're probably keeping it after closing, so that's not an expense that would be on the books if a non-owner was managing that business. So you get to add that cost back in as if it was profit, and any other silly expenses that the company might have purchased for your enjoyment. Your salary also gets considered. They will have to eventually replace you, so you don't get to add back the entire salary, but if you are under or overpaying yourself, they might adjust for that also.

Once you arrive at that number, your real annual profit with all the smoke and mirrors removed, the value of your business is basically that number, multiplied by the number of years one might expect it to continue at the present rate of growth. If your company has 15 employees, three million in recurring revenue, and 600k in EBITDA and add backs, you might get a multiplier of 4. If you're twice that size, you might get a multiplier of 5. If you've got 100 people and 8 figure revenue, you might be at 6x or more. So the napkin math tells us that your 15 employee company with 3 million in annual recurring revenue, and 600k in annual profit is probably worth something like two to three million dollars.

Notice I said recurring revenue. In our industry, one time projects and hardware sales are worth next to nothing, because there's no guarantee of any future revenue. Especially if you just had a great year, they will argue that it was a fluke, and there is no guarantee it will happen again, especially without you there to close the deals.

That's another reason why they often want the founder to stick around. You can do a deal where you get to walk away, but they will make you pay handsomely for the privilege of leaving. You can increase your valuation by reducing the buyer's anxiety. You can do that by agreeing to stick around and help for a while, and/or by taking some of the money in an earn out, which is based on the performance of the company's assets over time. You can also increase valuation by agreeing to an asset sale instead of a stock sale. This means that the liabilities stay with you, the seller, which is only a good idea if you're pretty sure there aren't any.

The magic in this process is that the buyer who completes the acquisition of another company is creating money out of thin air. Because her company is instantly larger, it potentially gets a bigger multiplier, but she also gets to put your revenue and earnings on her balance sheet, so the multiplier on your earnings is also increased. If you're doing smart deals that make sense, everyone is making money, but paradoxically the buyer is poised to make more money than anyone else.

If the buyer can manage a couple acquisitions each year, their multiplier will grow and grow until they reach a huge milestone - the IPO. When a company goes public, investors can trade shares easily, and an average company in the NASDAQ is cruising down the street with a multiplier of 30. Apple, Google, and Microsoft are all right there. The market expects those companies to last for a generation. Tesla's price to earnings ratio is over 60. Amazon's is 106. Think about that. The market thinks that Amazon will keep making money at the same rate for 106 years, and has already priced that in. If you think that's nuts, NVIDIA's P/E ratio is an astonishing 225. Which means if NVIDIA bought Berkshire Hathaway and managed to maintain their P/E ratio, theoretically, Berkshire Hathaway's comparatively modest 750 billion in market cap would become a cool 7 trillion as NVIDIA-Berkshire Hathaway at the moment the deal closed.

Of course, it's a silly example. If NVIDIA acquired Berkshire Hathaway, it would in reality take a lot of wind out of their sails. The reason they're getting such a crazy valuation is precisely because focused investing in the infrastructure that makes LLMs possible is speculated to be a very good investment, and tying up all of their cash and credit to buy the parent company of Geico would probably send the wrong message.

On the other hand, one time AOL bought Time Warner.

But this kind of multiplicative value creation happens in SMBs all day long. In fact, small business M&A is one of the best legal ways to create generational wealth. There is a voracious appetite for well constructed small businesses, and participating in mergers and acquisitions is one of the main reasons people get an MBA.

Once you get into that twilight stage, you start to evaluate decisions differently. Those holiday parties that cost a few thousand dollars? Multiply that cost by 4-6x. If you stop buying lunch for the office once a week, you might add tens of thousands of dollars to your LOI. Expenses get put on hold. The engineers can go to the conference in Vegas next year, but not this year for some ambiguous reason. And if you can land a new deal, oh man does that feel good. You start mentally multiplying everything in your head once you understand how this works. When you begin with the end in mind, you can start doing that sooner.

The other thing that became an obsession for me was MRR - monthly recurring revenue. I structured as much revenue as possible as a monthly payment so that I could max out this number. Even hardware and projects. I'd tell the customer that we'd just conveniently amortize the cost of their project into the 3 year agreement they're signing, because then I was making 5x as much money. Customer wants to order some new laptops? How about a zero interest "hardware as a service" agreement? Everything became a monthly payment. It's very attractive to do this if you're heading for the exit.

If you work for a small business that's in twilight, once you realize what might be going on in the owner's mind, you can usually spot behaviors that indicate they're thinking about selling, but if you run your business this way the entire time, cognizant that you've got a plan and a timeline that you're trying to execute against, your chances of success improve, and it will be less obvious to everyone when you start to get serious about making a deal.

Once we weeded through the private equity folks and a couple of low-ball offers, I made a good decision and began reaching out to my network in an effort to find a strategic buyer. It was important to me that the buyer paid us market value, but also that they knew what to do with the business. I wanted my employees and customers to be taken care of. So I called Robert DeMarzo, who everyone in the IT industry calls "Bobby D." We had worked together on the NexGen Cloud conferences for a few years, and I got to know him a little bit. He ran events for CRN/The Channel

Company back then, and now he's at Informa, which puts on the Channel Futures Leadership Summit and also Black Hat, a world famous conference for hackers where it's best to leave your cell phone powered off and nowhere near the conference center.

Bobby D gave me a few minutes of his time, pledged his support, and made two introductions. One was to a fellow I already knew. David Powell is a living legend in the MSP space, and it was silly that I hadn't discussed my plan with him yet. I fixed that, and he had some great ideas and really helped me understand the process and what to expect. Notably, he mentioned that if we were growing, we should ask buyers for "LQA" - last quarter annualized. Basically instead of just looking at the previous year, we should ask them to multiply the last quarter's earnings by four. The other introduction that he made for me was to Gary Pica, who has been through the M&A process several times, and now trains MSP owners to maximize the profitability and efficiency of their business.

Gary tried to talk me out of selling. He pushed hard, and he's an excellent salesman, but he wasn't able to undo 10 years of careful planning and execution in the course of a 30 minute call. When he saw my mind was fixed, he made two introductions, one to a potential buyer, and one to a business broker, George. George also made two introductions, one to a company that was rolling up MSPs all over the country, and another to the gentlemen who bought our business.

The diligence was intense, and George warned me in advance that the letter of intent, the LOI, was just the halfway mark. They dug into all kinds of aspects of the business, and it took months. The buyers, James and Dave, had been friends since third grade, and ran their business with tenacity, passion, and purpose. They were different in complementary ways, and I observed the way their styles manifested when I played against them in a game of table tennis.

James was all power shots. He put a little topspin on it, but unless I scraped the net or hit the edge of the table, he returned it fast and accurately in a straightforward fashion, moving me deftly, back and forth from forehand to backhand until I was tired and he was victorious.

Dave was all about spin, He held the paddle upside down, and would use side, back and top spin randomly whenever it suited him. I could never tell which way the ball was going to bounce.

Dave is a visionary. James is an integrator. Dave is creative. James is efficient. Together, I saw that they made each other better, and I suspected they could take my business farther than I could.

One of my customers was about to go public. Another of my customers had just been acquired by the largest public homebuilder in Japan. I had two of the largest escrow companies in Southern California, and a lot of the small ones. They were getting top tier customers and new market territory.

I was finally going to be able to buy a house. And a boat. And a convertible. And a new guitar. And play some golf without taking work calls between holes. I was about to begin really taking care of myself and my family for the first time in, well, ever.

It was incredibly gratifying to have outsiders value what we had built. There were flaws in our design, but they gave me a lot of credit for things that I wasn't sure if I had executed well, and that mattered to me. They admired what they bought and the people who built it for them. I started walking a little taller.

The assets performed well, and I was happy for them. I stayed there for two years, and did my best to take care of our customers and employees through the grip of the pandemic and for quite a while after things went back to normal. The day I resigned from that job to take an executive position at a different company, I remember pressing send on the email, and feeling a sort of catharsis. The tears came slowly at first, but then they started to flow freely. It was finished. Twelve years of my life, some of the best people I'd ever known, hard challenges and an incredible success story had all been in my grasp, and when I pushed that button, it unceremoniously ended. But it was supposed to. I thought about it, and I wasn't really sad. I experienced a profound emotional release when I realized that chapter of my life was really over. It felt a little like grief, but I was also letting go of a lot of anxiety. The plan worked. Everyone was OK. We did it.

The Irish Goodbye, at its core, is an elegant and subversive act of consideration. You're at a party, at the point in the evening when enough alcohol has been served that people are beginning to feel comfortable discussing politics and religion. The conversations blur into a low hum, and you find yourself thinking about home—the familiar comforts of pajamas and your bed. And suddenly, you ask yourself, "Why do I need to say goodbye?"

The half-hearted hugs, the performative and insincere "we should do this again soon" that everyone knows is a lie. You have a quiet power in this moment: the ability to slip away unnoticed, leaving the party intact, the mood undisturbed. No one's fun gets spoiled by your departure. You can avoid the social ritual of closure—why remind people that time is passing?

The Irish Goodbye isn't Irish like a leprechaun eating corned beef under a canopy of shamrocks. It's Irish like subtle rebellion, a rejection of the drawn-out, awkward farewell. It's not rude, it's efficient—a clean break. You intuitively know when it's time to step away, to leave while the story continues without you. And that's the beauty of it. The party goes on for everyone else, and you're free.

12

WALKING EACH OTHER HOME

sometimes
we need others to give us permission
to do what we know we need to do, to
give us validation to do what we
want to do but for whatever reason,
 can't.

and so we go on
trusting
and so we go on
recognizing + honoring
our needs and the needs of others
and so we go on
walking each other home

It is a dance.

- Durga Sánchez

My favorite helpdesk ticket of all time was a report that a computer was shutting down when the end user left the room. "The computer knows when I am here," the user explained. "It turns off when I stop paying attention to it, and if I don't remember to save, I often lose all my work. If I go to the bathroom and come back, I can hear it powering on when I walk back to my desk. It's driving me nuts."

In IT support, there are a couple of unfortunate acronyms used to describe situations when the user is the problem. If you ever hear an IT person refer to an ID Ten T error, they're calling you mean names. It makes more sense when you write it as ID10T.

PEBKAC is another one I've heard. It stands for "Problem Exists Between Keyboard And Chair" — in other words, the issue is the person, not the system. Frequently this is both an unfortunate way to talk about a paying customer and an accurate diagnosis.

In this case, it wasn't either of those things. The user had connected her desktop computer to a power outlet that was a switched outlet, and in an effort to save electricity, the company had installed new energy efficient motion sensing switches. It might have worked flawlessly if she had plugged in a lamp or a fan, but since she plugged in a computer, it "knew" when she walked out of the room, and shut off power to the device. When she walked back in, the motion sensor on the wall would switch on and restore power to the device. She was completely right, and I'm embarrassed to admit that it took us three service calls to resolve that. I think someone swapped the entire computer before we figured it out.

I remember once a technician who returned from a service call started complaining loudly about how stupid the customer was, and how easy it was to solve their issue.

"Which customer are you returning from," I asked?

It was a law firm.

"Cool, and I assume you know how to file a subpoena? What's the basic idea in the seventh amendment to the Constitution?"

He stared back at me as I explained, "They know how to do things that you don't know how to do, and you know how to do things that they don't know how to do. That means we should be friends, right? You should be grateful that there is something you know how to do that they know how to pay for, because if anyone relied on you for legal advice, they'd probably wind up in jail."

Like I said, I wasn't particularly easy to work with.

It's true that sometimes the problem exists between the keyboard and the chair, but I'd like to reclaim this acronym. More often than not it's also the passion, the power, the potential, and the promise. More often than not it's where you find a reason to persist. The purpose of technology is to serve the person sitting in that chair, and for that person, each moment of work matters.

I can remember being in fourth grade, terrified of fifth grade. Sure, I'd been able to keep up the farce until this point, but maybe after summer vacation it would start to become obvious that I didn't belong. Long division with remainders made perfect sense to me, but I looked at my older friend's math book, and multiplying and dividing fractions seemed way beyond my abilities. I was an anxious kid. Still am, I guess.

One peculiarity that I've noticed about success is that as I've climbed the ladder, I keep meeting other people who are successful, and once I get to know them, most of them seem about as confident that they belong in their station as I was that I could handle the 5th grade. Some people are skilled at strutting around like corporate peacocks, making an implausible show of cultivated arrogance, but most successful people simply learn to manufacture the necessary confidence to maintain their lifestyle.

At the top of the food chain, I was surprised to discover that no one really seems to know what they're doing—they're just much better at pretending they do. We're really all just anxious children, scared that someone will figure out we never should have passed the fourth grade. Conference rooms full of Billy Madisons in expensive suits. I'm more than halfway through life, and I still feel like a dumb kid most of the time. Like someday maybe I'll figure out the things that only grownups know.

I'm mentioning this because I spent a lot of my life wrestling with impostor syndrome, worrying about what other people think, anxious that I wouldn't be able to perform at the next required level of proficiency. I didn't think I would be able to command the attention of a boardroom, manage thousands of people and devices, captivate an audience of thousands, defend against existential cyberthreats, keep national security secrets, advise government officials, or convince a beautiful woman to marry me until I went out and did all of those things.

There's a book that a friend recommended to me called *The Courage To Be Disliked*. One of my favorite chapters explains that no one cares what you look like. We all spend absurd amounts of time and energy cultivating and manifesting our physical appearances, but to what end? Everyone is already preoccupied with their own problems. No one is going to remember in a couple days that you were walking around with a little mustard stain on your shirt, or that you have a weird mole under your nose. They probably didn't notice it to begin with, unless you drew attention to it. Don't believe me? Think about someone else who was present in the last meeting you had. What color was the other person's shirt? Yeah, maybe you got that one, maybe, but now tell me what that person was wearing the previous time you met with them? What about the time before that? Unless they showed up in a Halloween costume, your brain probably discarded almost all of the information it gathered about their appearance, and you totally missed that mole, pimple, or cold sore that they were thinking about the entire time.

But if you're like me, you lie awake at night, dissecting your conversations, wondering and worrying about how you were perceived. You buy nice clothes and find a competent barber, because you hope to at least blend in, but the truth is that nobody cares what you look like. There's a lot of freedom in that.

A couple other things I need to get off my chest. I started a business with my friends, and it did not make us become better friends. That really wasn't what I intended. As I've admitted, I was intense and difficult, sardonic, argumentative and stubborn. People say you shouldn't start a business with your friends, and now I understand why they say that. I still care about those guys, and I hope someday they will forgive me for the ways I wounded them along our journey. Even though we largely succeeded in our objective, we're not really part of each other's lives anymore.

Maybe we just spent too much time together, and they're ready to be around people who are more fun or kind or positive or entertaining. It's a little weird for me writing this, knowing that they'll probably read it. I don't like letting go of friendships, especially with people I really respect. Count the cost of that when you consider who you're going to work with. I think we each went out of our way to be fair to each other, and by and large I would say we were good business partners, but running a business together ultimately drove us apart. It's a lot of drama and stress while it's all happening, and the potential exists that you will wear out those friendships with anxiety, anger, and bad decisions, despite your best intentions.

On the other side of the spectrum, being the boss meant that I got to pick most of the people I worked with every day, which brought me great joy. To spot the potential in people and help them learn how to use it was an honor. I spent some of the best years of my life with people I got to choose. How many people can say the same? I'm not sure the people who worked for me always understood how much I cared about them, or appreciated how hard it was to always pay them on time, but I think of them often and smile when I hear about their successes. I hope they can take the hard won knowledge we learned together in those years and be wildly successful in business and life.

When the business was new, we would celebrate little wins with what we called "balcony time." If one of us sold a few laptops or we picked up a new account, we would toast on our tiny balcony with some cheap whiskey poured over a gigantic ice cube. It was a moment of joy in a sea of long and hard days. Later on we had higher thresholds for celebration and better liquor, but it's important to feel like you're in it with people who are invested in you and in your mutual success. Starting traditions is a tried and true way to build culture.

One of the things that seemed to move us forward and beyond some obstacles was getting away for a couple days and talking strategically about what we were doing next. We did this about once a year, and it was always time well spent.

I realized that a skill I picked up in a public speaking class was also an effective way for me to solve business problems—just keep talking until you find the answer. Often, in the process of explaining a problem to one of my partners, the solution would come out of my mouth in one of the next sentences, even if I had been thinking about it by myself unsuccessfully for hours. Talking things out with them was extremely helpful to me, though it probably seemed strange to them that I would demand their time and then proceed to monologue until the answer presented itself.

I don't know why it's like that, but for me it is. My former partners are both good listeners, and I've learned that there is something in the act of talking through a problem or opportunity that makes your synapses fire differently. Maybe that's why people figure things out in therapy.

I remember the hard times, the passionate arguments about things that really didn't end up mattering ultimately, but I also feel so much profound gratitude to both of them. I would have never had the confidence to start that business without them standing next to me, believing in us. Without them dreaming about the future with me over dim sum and charcuterie, working hard together to make that future become a reality, a lot of wonderful things in my life never would have happened.

Business, like life, is about relationships, not competition. People should come before everything else, especially technology, which is just a means to an end. Most relationship problems stem from feelings of inferiority, and those feelings are something you've built up in your mind, because you're scared, but so is everyone else. Lead with love, but be brave. You must not lose your daring. People are depending on you to be daring.

You also don't need to compare yourself to anyone. Stop doing that. Seriously, stop it. Instead, contribute. Build something great. Live in the moment. Care about the right things. Be strategic about the things you can control, and let the rest of it go. I think it's important to treat people with kindness and respect, but if you can learn to be content without validation from others, you'll find yourself freer than you ever imagined. When you grow into a new phase of life, it's unsettling and liberating, all at once. If I can do it, so can you. I believe in you.

ACKNOWLEDGEMENTS

Kelly, you are the love of my life, and my favorite secret to all of our success. Thank you for making me a Dad and giving me the reasons and courage to do all of this. I did it for you. I love you.

Boys, I hope you read this someday and that it will put some things in context for you. Your mom and I worked hard to make things a little easier for you. Pay it forward by being kind and respectful to people who don't have it as easy. I love you and I'm proud of you.

Mom and Dad, I hope I can be as positive an influence on your grandchildren as you have been for me. Your fingerprints are all over this book.

To the MSP Community, I know you will relate to the stories in this book, and I hope you find something here that inspires you to make and tell your own story.

Roger, I'm struggling to count the number of times I've hired you, and every time it was a good decision. I'm so proud of the person you've become.

Chris, Chad, Roger, Richard, Danny, Jennifer, Victor, Ross, Brandon, Cameron, Kyle, Katie, Zach, Ashley, Nathan, Peter,

Acknowledgements

Jon, Lawrence, Will, Steven, Stephen, Dan, James, Dave, Roberta, Skip, Rob, John, Aaron, Durga, Laurie, Taurean, Jim, Barry, Brad, Larry, Adam, Melissa, Bret, Brandon, Shawn, CJ, Gilbert, Michael, Kevin, Brian, Pat, Andy, Brent, Greg, Christopher, and Tim, working with you has made me a better human. Thank you for being part of my life and for investing in me.

Bret, Aaron, and Tom, thanks for reading my draft and giving me valuable feedback.

Phil Putnam, this book only came together for me after I saw how you did it. I'm walking in your footsteps now. I hope I've left enough snark in it to properly entertain you.

Guy Kawasaki, Karl Palachuk, and Dr. Ivan Misner, I learned things from you that changed the trajectory of my life. Thank you for your ideas and for writing them down.

Darrin, thank you for being my friend and pastor for almost thirty years. You're going to be an incredible grandpa.

Carl and Paul, thanks for still wanting to make music with me after all these years. I love all of the hideous beauty we've created together.

Tom Willett, when you told me I would be successful someday, it's the first time I believed that about myself. I'm trying to lead with bravery and love, like you taught me.

www.ingramcontent.com/pod-product-compliance
Lightning Source LLC
Chambersburg PA
CBHW031423210526
45464CB00005B/2018